BEHIND TI

Ferdinand Dennis was born in Jamaica in 1956
and came to Britain at an early age. He was
educated at Rutherford Comprehensive, the University of Leicester where he studied sociology,
and Birkbeck College, London where he obtained
his M.Sc. He has worked as an educational
researcher, and been a university lecturer in
Nigeria. He now works as a freelance journalist –
he has broadcast a number of programmes with
the BBC and has contributed to many newspapers
and journals including *The Guardian*, *City Limits*
and *The Listener*. He has travelled widely in
Africa, and now lives in London.

FERDINAND DENNIS

BEHIND
THE
FRONTLINES

Journey into Afro-Britain

LONDON
VICTOR GOLLANCZ LTD
1988

First published in Great Britain 1988
by Victor Gollancz Ltd,
14 Henrietta Street, London WC2E 8QJ

First published in Gollancz Paperbacks 1988

British Library Cataloguing in Publication Data
Dennis, Ferdinand, *1956–*
    Behind the frontlines : journey into
    Afro-Britain.
    1. England. West Indians. Social life
    I. Title
    942.085′8

ISBN 0–575–04098–X
ISBN 0–575–04327–X Pbk

Typeset at The Spartan Press Limited,
Lymington, Hants
and printed in Finland by Werner Södeström OY

FOR MY FATHER, J. R. DENNIS

Contents

Foreword

In the winter of 1987 I made a journey which took me from my home in London to Liverpool, Sheffield, Birmingham, Cardiff, Bristol, and for an unscheduled day to Bath. On returning to London I paid several visits to Brixton. The purpose of my journey was to write a travelogue about black Britain (here I use this problematic term "black" only in relation to people of African descent). "Behind the Frontlines" is the result.

It is not a political, sociological or race relations tract. Rather, it records my encounters, impressions and conversations along the way. Most black communities have a physical space which is commonly known as the "frontline", or simply "the line". These are usually the flashpoints for conflicts with the law. Frontlines, though, are also vital creative places, and an important influence on the frontline is Rastafarianism. Its language, its style, its concerns were, for me, the most engaging part of my journey. But, as the title implies, I went behind the frontlines. And each city yielded something different. In Liverpool, for instance, it was the old African sailors; in Birmingham, the black churches, in Bristol, old West Indian sailors. The differences in the views of the stable and volatile were not always so great as I expected. But that is part of the pleasure of any journey: constant surprise.

Throughout my trip, I tried as much as possible to speak

to ordinary folks: people whose opinions would normally go unrecorded. Some names have been changed, especially where I thought certain remarks might have adverse repercussions on the speaker.

Since completing the trip a number of changes have occurred in one or two cities. But they do not fundamentally affect the book's contents. Black life goes on.

I am indebted to BBC Radio Four for whom I was researching the series "Journey Round my People" when the idea of this book was born. My thanks to those whose warm hospitality made my journey over those cold months an unforgettable experience, in particular Tunde Zack-Williams, Glen Jordan and Cathy and Frank Waite. And a very special thanks to Audrey West for her patience and tolerance during the writing of this book.

F. D.
February 1988

Acknowledgements

The Author gratefully acknowledges
the financial assistance
of The Cadbury Trust
during the writing of this book.

F. D.

BEHIND THE FRONTLINES

"For I am a direct descendant of slaves, too near to the actual enterprise to believe that its echoes are over with the reign of emancipation. Moreover, I am a direct descendant of Prospero worshipping in the same temple of endeavour, using his legacy of language – not to curse our meeting – but to push it further, reminding the descendants on both sides that what's done is done, and can only be seen as a soil from which other gifts, or the same gift endowed with different meanings, may grow towards a future which is colonised by our acts in this moment, but which must always remain open."

George Lamming, *The Pleasures of Exile*

"The contradictory violence of our reactions and the explosions of our intimate selves and our history all began as a rejection of the petrified forms oppressing us; now we are attempting to resolve them by creating a society which is not ruled by lies and betrayals, avarice and violence and dissimulation."

Octavio Paz, *The Labyrinth of Solitude*

1. The Outward Journey

The New Year, just a week old, stretched in front of me like a vast uncharted sea. I sat in the bar at Euston station contemplating the journey ahead. Liverpool was to be my first stop. The still, grey sky under which I'd travelled to the station now seemed portentous. All the stories I'd heard about the crippling severity of northern winters replayed in my mind. I shivered and sipped my lager. In the bar post-Christmas depression prevailed. It was most visible in the solitary paper-chain which hung limply on a far wall.

A grizzly-faced old man asked to share my table. He placed a full pint of bitter on it. Then he sat down ceremoniously, hitching his trousers. Short and scruffily dressed, he had about him an air of dereliction like a condemned building. In one gulp, he swallowed a third of his drink and smacked his lips. Then he leant towards me and declared: "I'm a happy man. You know why I'm a happy man?" He spoke with a Yorkshire accent.

I shook my head.

"Because I'm free, and I've got two kids. Both grown up. I've just been to see 'em."

He spoke loudly. Four labourers at the next table began to take interest in him and me, his captive listener. One had vaguely Anglo-Asian features, and was burly and wore a battle-green fatigue-jacket. He smiled sympathetically at me. I returned a grin of hopelessness.

"You know," the old man said, suddenly lowering his voice, "three years ago I went home from work. Used to work in the mines then. Don't any more. Not many people do any more. Went home to me wife, walked into our bedroom and there she was below another man."

He paused, his face assumed an expression of bewilderment and pain. He stared into the now half-empty glass, as if it contained all the intimate memories of that moment of betrayal.

"Walked straight out, I did," he continued. "Used to save a bit of money every week. Two quid. A lot in those days. Went right to the bank, told the manager I wanted everything. The whole lot. And that was the last time I saw Leeds."

He took a long swig and asked: "Tell you what'd make me a happier man?" He looked at me probingly, as if genuinely needing my permission to proceed. "I'll tell you," he said. "To hear that my wife is dead. That'd be it for me. Real good." With another swig he had finished the glass. He rose and sauntered towards the bar.

"A mate of yours?" the Anglo-Asian shouted across to me, grinning. His mates roared with laughter. I smiled and shrugged.

I'd begun reading a magazine when I heard a commotion. It was the old man. He was pestering a pretty, dark-haired barmaid. In a slurred voice, he was telling her: "You look just like my wife when she was young. Just like 'er." The girl was embarrassed. Then the barman intervened. With a no-nonsense expression he marched the old man out. As they passed, the Anglo-Asian said: "'Ere, you should call his wife. Tell 'er to come for him." His friends howled with laughter at this masterly piece of heartless wit.

I was seated near the same group of men on the Liverpool train. It seemed that they were migrant workers returning to their northern homes for a few days' break. They drank innumerable cans of McEwan's Export Lager and made ribald remarks at any woman who passed by.

Outside, the frozen landscape of lifeless trees became monotonous and I dozed off. I awoke to the same voices, their raucous laughter, their table a pool of empty cans. Then a strange thing happened. One of the men enquired about somebody called Pete. The Asian replied incredulously: "You haven't heard!"

Another member of the group said: "Go on, you're joking. Everyone knows what 'appened to Pete."

"If I had I wouldn't be asking, you berk," the man who'd enquired replied.

"Well 'e's dead, ain't he," the Anglo-Asian said.

"What?"

"Yeah, D-E-A-D. Dead."

"Blimey! Last time I saw 'im he had a nice little earner."

"Yeah, it was a nice little earner," the Anglo-Asian said. "But 'e 'ad to do a fourteen-hour day, seven-day week, with a three-day break every six weeks. All he could do was sleep when 'e got a break. One day 'e didn't go in. Probably too knackered. When he made it in next day, 'e was given his cards. Just like that."

"Blimey! So how did he die?"

"Car accident. You know that old banger he used to drive. Wrapped it round a lamp-post. He was pissed out of his head. Couldn't go home, I heard. His wife, five bleeding kids. Couldn't face them, I heard."

There was no more laughter after that. A sober silence settled amongst them, as if death itself had sat with them.

And I remembered the wretched old man back in the bar, their heartless laughter. Perhaps they had been laughing at a possible version of their own future. Perhaps they had laughed out of fear.

2. Liverpool: Sins of the Fathers

It was Saturday morning and Liverpool city centre was already crowded with shoppers. The air was sharp and damp, the sky overcast. A few stray gulls circled above, as if searching for the sea or the River Mersey, their cries drowned in the noise below. As I waited at a pedestrian crossing, a woman complained to her companion about the absence of buses. "Diabolical it is," she said. "Imagine them striking on a Saturday." Like many others I'd got to the city centre by taxi.

The main shopping precinct could have been of any major provincial British city but, beyond the familiar shop fronts, Liverpool comes into its own. The city is replete with centuries-old buildings which have lost their grandeur. They are coated with grime and afflicted with decay. In gloomily narrow streets, they look sad; in open spaces, tragic, and next to the steel-and-glass of modern structures, pathetic. These architectural wrecks were once monuments to an age of prosperity. Now they stand as disturbingly ugly symbols of decline.

Liverpool once rivalled London in its opulence, boasting more millionaires than any other part of Britain. Sea trade was the source of Liverpool's growth. In the latter part of the nineteenth century, it was the exit point for millions of British emigrants heading for Australia and the United States of America.

But before that, this blighted city thrived on another type of human cargo: African slaves. In fact, Liverpool's former greatness was derived almost entirely from its involvement in what the poet William Cowper described as "cargoes of despair". Its founding father, Thomas Johnson, was a slave merchant. So too were most of its important historical figures. In the eighteenth century, through a mixture of ingenuity, aggression and greed, Liverpool grew from an insignificant port to become Europe's leading slave-trading port. The first recorded voyage was undertaken by *The Liverpool Merchant*. The slaves were delivered to Barbados. There was no stopping the Liverpool traders after that. By mid-century, they had surpassed those of Bristol and London. The entire city participated, from attorneys to barbers. A local historian wrote in 1795: "Almost every man in Liverpool is a merchant, and he who cannot send a bale will send a bandbox . . . the attractive African meteor has . . . so dazzled their ideas that almost every order of people is interested in a Guinea cargo."

The Liverpool brand, DD, became known as a guarantee of quality. Burnt into the cheeks, forehead, shoulders, backs or buttocks of captive Africans, it was a mark that the Africans being sold were "Prime healthy Negroes". One way of ensuring prime quality was to purchase children. In 1797, the master of *The Earl of Liverpool*, owned by Thomas Leyland, was instructed: "In your selection of the slave we desire you will not purchase any exceeding eighteen to twenty years of age, well formed and free of any disorder."

All manner of brutalities were committed in the pursuit of profit. Over a century earlier, in 1674, a captain of the ironically named *Black Joke* flogged to death a one-year-old child for refusing food. Its mother was forced to throw the corpse overboard. And profits could be extraordinarily high, as much as 300 per cent in some instances, though, on average, an investment in a slave ship returned profits of 10 per cent.

Profits from slavery formed the basis of Liverpool's banking system, financed the cotton industry in nearby Manchester and generally built up the city. After the abolition of the slave trade, Liverpool became the principal port for the importation of slave-grown cotton from the United States for the cotton mills of Manchester.

The slave trade, of course, benefitted the whole of Britain. Not all, though, appreciated that. George Frederick Cooke, an eighteenth-century tragedian, was one. Booed and hissed by a Liverpool theatre audience one night, he retorted: "I have not come here to be insulted by a set of wretches, of which every brick in your infernal town is cemented with an African's blood." Cooke's dissatisfied audience fell silent. And it is a silence which still seems to pervade Liverpool today. The past is not only another country, it is one too far away to be seen.

The city's museum has only a minor exhibition on the slave trade. Situated to the right of the entrance, it is easily overlooked by visitors. Its size and location hint at a desire to sanitise Liverpool's history, to purge the records. Another Liverpool Museum does not even bother to acknowledge the trade's existence. The Maritime Museum is part of new Liverpool. Situated in the Albert Dock, its contents are all about Liverpool's role in the nineteenth-century exodus to the Americas and Australasia. After strolling around, I spoke to one of the museum guards. Stocky and ruddy-faced, he was an ex-sailor. He'd been to most West African ports and numerous Caribbean islands. The Maritime Museum, he said, was a "great idea", because "without the port there wouldn't be any Liverpool. Not as we know it anyway." A union contact had landed him the job. Most of the museum guards had come through the Seamen's Union. "Better than the dole," he said, which is where he'd languished for two years after leaving the sea.

He was a pleasant, talkative man, and I asked him why there was no mention of the slave trade. He scratched his head and replied: "The Albert Dock was built long after that." An uncomfortable silence followed.

But the slave trade did exist. Liverpool's long established black community – Britain's oldest – was living evidence. After the Maritime Museum, I headed for Liverpool 8, or Toxteth.

Vince Taylor lived in a two-storey terraced house in Liverpool 8. He came from Freetown, Sierra Leone. His surname, Taylor, revealed a lot about him. Freetown was founded by English abolitionists in 1787 to resettle freed slaves from Jamaica, Nova Scotia and London. British names like Taylor, Williams and Cole are common there.

His wife answered the door. She was light-complexioned and had jet-black hair and a hammer-shaped nose. Her eyes were large and black and sad.

She showed me into a tiny living-room. The walls were bare, but for two West African masks. A gas fire hissed and blazed. On the mantelpiece were photographs of two children and a smiling couple. The bay window was filled by a huge television and video. Though blank, the screen dominated the room, where three men sat. Vince rose from the armchair and we shook hands. His was soft and moist, his handshake limp. He was short and wiry and had a moon-shaped scar below his left eye.

I explained that I'd got his address from his cousin, Joe, in whose flat I was staying. Joe, an old friend of mine, was out of the country. Vince said he had been expecting me and introduced me to his friends seated on the sofa and asked his wife to make tea. "No coffee," he said apologetically.

"Funny place to write about. Liverpool," Vince said. "Nothing happens up 'ere."

"Got the best football teams," one of the men said. He'd been introduced to me as Lenny, and was much older than Vince or the third man.

"What d'you know 'bout football!" Vince said reprovingly.

I explained that I would be visiting other cities as well. My aim was to write about black people, or people of African descent. Liverpool was an obvious stop because of its age-old black community. But my explanation only drew blank responses. Foolishly, perhaps, I'd expected a conversation about the quality of black life in Liverpool. Instead, Vince and Lenny, in whom I detected a Caribbean accent, began arguing about football. I was left to talk to Steve. He had a large, smooth, dark face, and, I learnt, was also a Sierra Leonean.

Steve had only been in Britain for six months. In spite of the gas fire, he complained about the cold. He was serious: he hadn't taken off his padded bomber jacket, and played with his thick gloves, as if resisting the temptation to put them on.

After tea, Vince suggested we went to the pub. All agreed. Before we left, the two children who were in the photograph came in. The older, a girl, was darker than Vince, but had his heavy eyelids. The boy had his mother's complexion and her obtrusive nose. "You wouldn't believe they're brother and sister, would you?" Vince said to me. I guessed he was referring to their contrasting complexions, and remarked on it. "That's Liverpool for you, black people up here are so mixed up, you're never sure what the kids are gonna look like."

As we walked down the street, he told me of a Liverpool woman who could pass for white. Determined to leave Liverpool 8, she married a white man. But the husband deserted her when she gave birth to a brown-skinned, curly-haired baby. Now she is back in Liverpool 8.

Vince and Steve began talking in their Sierra Leone creole, something about the weather. I fell into step with Lenny. Maybe it was his discovery that we were both Jamaicans, or an attempt to distract himself from the now biting cold – whatever it was, he talked non-stop.

Lenny was visiting Vince that afternoon because of an incident earlier that morning. He had been drinking the previous night. Too drunk to go home, he stopped at a friend's house. The friend was away, but his woman allowed him to stay there. His friend often travelled and the woman's hospitality wasn't unusual. He slept for some hours and woke up with the dawn, feeling ravenously hungry. He went to the woman's bedroom, intending to ask if he could help himself to some bread. The door was open, so he entered. Unknown to Lenny, his friend had returned and gone straight to bed. When his friend saw him, he got the wrong idea and gave Lenny a thorough beating before throwing him out. "Wouldn't believe me at-aall," said an aggrieved Lenny. "Accuse me of sexing his lady friend behind his back. Me, his good friend. Some people really bad-minded."

The pub was a semi-dilapidated, redbrick building on a corner site. It was surprisingly quiet for a Saturday afternoon. Three girls talking to the barmaid and a couple playing pool were the only customers. I bought a round of drinks. Lenny took his lager with shaking hands and revealed that he hadn't eaten in four days. "Lager is all right for me, though," he said. "Wine and whisky, they're what I keep away from when I haven't eaten."

"Why?" asked Steve.

"Oh, lager I can handle. But wine and whisky drive me crazy. They just make me want sex. Get me into trouble a whole heapa times, man."

Vince gave me a long-suffering look. He asked again why I'd chosen Liverpool as one of the cities to write about, and suggested the riots. I said Liverpool had always struck me as being an interesting place, long before the '81 and '85 riots. I wanted to see the neighbourhood when it wasn't rioting, just getting on with life and living.

"There's a lotta life round here all right," said Vince. "But not much living. Nearly everyone's on the dole."

"Are you?"

"Me? I haven't had a proper job in ten years. Not looking for one either."

Vince laughed. Not at his own words, but at Lenny, whose eyes had become glassy, as if he'd only been a sip away from drunkenness. He was humming a tune and stroking his glass.

Vince commented to Steve in Creole which, despite its similarity to the Jamaican dialect, I found difficult to follow.

Looking around the pub, I noticed a small stage beyond the pool players. Its backdrop was a green fluorescent outline of the African continent. It seemed an unusual sight, the shape of Africa decorating an English pub. I went to take a closer look. Afterwards I stopped to watch the pool game. The male player was tall and skinny and moved with a painful slowness. His opponent was in her late teens or early twenties. Her only concession to femininity was a head of unkempt strands of plaited extensions.

As I stood watching she strode up to me with a masculine

swagger and asked: "Can you play pool?" Her eyes, set in a square handsome face, remained fixed on the table.

"I've played a few times."

"Good. I'll give you a game after I've beaten JJ."

She spoke with a broad Liverpool accent and exuded a brash confidence. Her oponent, JJ, heard her, looked up and grinned through his thick, black beard.

She introduced herself as Vicky. Vicky was clearly exasperated with JJ's slowness. Between shots he circled the table at least twice, studying it like a chess-player. And he took each shot with infinite delicacy.

"This is pool, JJ, not snooker," Vicky shouted in annoyance. But JJ ignored her and played on at his ponderous, if effective, pace. "That man'd give a headache to a Paracetamol," Vicky said, as JJ cleared the table. He won the game and she challenged him to another. Vicky's continued abuse of JJ only seemed to inspire him. She didn't get much chance to show off her skills. She had the time to talk and asked me where I came from. My answer left her unimpressed.

She said proudly: "I'm not from round here. I've only been here eight years."

"Where were you before?"

"America. That's where I was born. Me father is still there. He used to be in the Air Force and was based over here for a bit."

I must have looked sceptical, because to prove her claim she produced a US passport from her back pocket. "See, I can get out anytime I want," she said, waving the passport in my face like a child with a new toy trying to arouse envy in a friend. "I'm an American citizen. 'Orrible place this."

"So what's keeping you here?"

"Me mother. She's not well. Gotta look after her. Sell a bit of ganja on the side as well. 'Elps pay the rent. As soon as she pops it, I'll be off."

Such innocence! Such openness, and to a total stranger. It was as though she regarded her American passport as an inviolable protector. It gave her an unbreachable confidence. She could say whatever she wanted and to whoever she wanted. Because she could "get out anytime". But beyond the American-inspired bravado she was a dutiful daughter.

"Is he your boyfriend, then," I said, nodding at JJ.

"Who, JJ? Don't insult me," she said with mock indignation. She turned away from the table and lowered her voice. "He's sick you know." She twisted her forefinger on her temple. "Comes from Uganda. Used to drive a taxi. One night he picked up four white boys. They wouldn't pay the fare. They beat him up real bad. Over in the North End. Everybody feels sorry for JJ. Not me, though." She turned and shouted, "Isn't that right JJ?"

JJ gave her a quizzical glance, then returned his attention to the table and potted a ball. It signalled the end of the game and Vicky's defeat.

At the start of the next game, I left to rejoin my companions. Vince and Lenny were locked in a debate about whether the American boxer, Mike Tyson, was merely a media hype. Steve, pensive and distant, was staring at the frosted glass window. Their glasses were empty, so I offered to buy another round. Vince's smile of acceptance also revealed embarrassment, apology. He produced a pound coin as a contribution, and Steve a fifty-pence piece. Lenny simply grinned. I refused their money, realising that it was probably all they had between them. Three grown men broke on a Saturday afternoon! It was my first glimpse of northern poverty.

Steve perked up with his second drink. We got talking and I learnt he was an ex-sailor. Bored with sea life, he had jumped ship six months earlier. His ambition was to study electronics. But he needed a job to pay for the college fees and this was proving difficult to obtain. To compound his problems, as part of his strategy for legalising his stay, he'd married a local white girl. She was three months pregnant and they lived in one room. He'd thought of looking for work beyond Liverpool, but his wife objected. She'd even threatened to report him to the immigration authorities if he left.

I now understood why he appeared so withdrawn, almost despondent. I offered my sympathy.

The pub closed while we drank. But no one made an effort to drink up. In fact, more customers came after closing time. All black men, they greeted the white barmaid with familiarity. A trio occupied the neighbouring table and began a game of dominoes. Vince joined them.

I promised to call on Vince again, and left with Steve. It was dark outside and the temperature had dropped further. Before parting, Steve pointed me in the general direction of a cab route. We shook hands and he thanked me. For the drinks? For listening to his story? I said I hoped things worked out for the better. He thanked me again and walked away, hands in pockets, head lowered; back to his pregnant wife, his wretched single room.

Nearing Upper Parliament Street, I became aware of something I'd seen before. A street-name plaque was coloured red, gold and green over the black lettering. So was the next and the next.

Red, gold, green and black are the colours of the Rastafarian movement. It emerged in the poor urban districts of the Jamaican capital, Kingston, in the 1930s. The central ideas of this politico-religious cult are that the late Haile Selassie, former Ethiopian Emperor, is God or Jah, and that the descendants of freed African slaves in the West should be repatriated back to Africa.

The repatriation of people at least four hundred years removed from Africa may seem bizarre. But in the interwar years, Marcus Garvey, a Jamaican, built up the largest mass black movement in the twentieth century on just such an objective. His organisation had members throughout North and South America, the Caribbean and Africa. It even bought ships and negotiated for land with the Liberian government. His success in mobilising millions of Afro-Americans and Afro-Caribbeans had made him a legendary figure in history of people of African descent. The legend began when the Rastas adopted Garvey as a leader comparable to Moses. And his back-to-Africa ambition became a fundamental tenet in Rasta ideology. Many modern-day Rastas, however, favour a spiritual return to Africa, if only because the physical return has proved so difficult to achieve.

In the 1970s Rastafarianism exploded amongst the children of Afro-Caribbean immigrants. They adopted the Rasta hairstyle – dreadlocks – spoke in Rasta idiom, worshipped Haile Selassie, and read their Bibles through clouds of ganja smoke. They lived Rasta. Sociologists explained the phenomenon as a symptom of an identity crisis born of rejection. Born in Britain but alienated from it, these Rasta converts were seen as filling a vacuum created by being in, but not of, British society. Rasta, which had started life as an ideology of the displaced, became an ideology of the rejected.

The movement's influence went beyond black youngsters. Jamaican reggae music, played mainly by Rastas, became popular. It helped to revitalise a stagnant pop industry that was still mourning the break-up of the Beatles – a Liverpool group. Bob Marley, reggae's most famous ambassador, became a hero to generations of white youths. White musicians paid the ultimate compliment when they began imitating the music, reggae de blanc, as one mega-group described it. Some white youngsters even grew dreadlocks. And the red, gold and green entered the mainstream of popular culture.

I recall talking to a magazine designer in the early Eighties. She observed that as an art student she'd been discouraged from using bold colours. Combinations of colours like red, gold and green were considered gaudy. But in the late Seventies these colours were suddenly considered chic. It was she who made the connection with the Rastafarian movement and the increasing popularity of reggae music.

Red, gold and green, then, signify a people in historical exile, a people yearning for a land from which Liverpool's founding father, Thomas Johnson, had played no small part in forcefully removing them.

The paint-work had been hastily done, like graffiti. And it seemed to begin at the boundary of Liverpool 8, as if intended to distinguish it from the rest of the city. Why, I wondered, would anyone want to identify a neighbourhood in an English provincial city with a movement which regards the West, Britain in particular, as a place of exile, as Babylon? But Liverpool isn't just any English city. Its past distinguishes it.

It all seemed like more than mere coincidence. The coloured street signs intrigued me. There and then I decided to make my stay in Liverpool a search for the artist responsible.

On Sunday the temperature plunged below freezing point. Car locks had to be defrosted before they could be opened. No amount of clothing seemed adequate protection from the cold. But Liverpool and north-west England were fortunate. Other parts of Britain, particularly the south, suffered from snow storms. The weather, usually a national obsession, became a national mania. It dominated all news reports. Alarmed concern for the aged was voiced by care workers and politicians. Several old-age pensioners died of hypothermia in one day.

I left the flat where I was staying only once, to buy newspapers and cigarettes. By nightfall the snow had reached Liverpool, and I headed for the Caribbean Cultural Centre, which seemed a good place to start. I made my way along Upper Parliament Street, which runs from the docks past the Anglican Cathedral and into Liverpool South. Parts of it are lined with tall, old houses. Their splendour lost, they retain a certain elegance beneath the uniform grey and blue paint favoured by housing associations. They now serve as low-rent flats for workers, the unemployed, single parents and students. Liverpool University is nearby.

The Caribbean Cultural Centre is on the Toxteth side of Upper Parliament Street. A low, redbrick building, its grounds are large enough for a cricket pitch and basketball court. As I entered it, I was immediately greeted by a chorus of Barbadian accents. I knocked on a door to my right, the chorus stopped abruptly, and I was ordered to enter. Four men occupied a small office that stank of rum and cigar smoke. I introduced myself to a man seated at a desk. He had a long, rubbery face, reddish complexion, and sleepy eyes. With his worn-looking check jacket, he looked like a poorly paid estate keeper. This was Eustace, the centre's warden.

On learning that I was Jamaican, he offered me a drink of rum. The smooth, dark Barbadian rum, drunk from a paper cup, gave me an exhilarating warmth. My arrival had interrupted the conversation and they were keen to resume.

A brown-skinned man who had been introduced as Ron was most eager. He was the cigar smoker and his stomach protruded out of a ragged sheepskin coat.

"Now all right," Ron said to the others. "'E come from Jamaica. Let's 'ear what 'e think 'bout it." He turned to me and said: "We was talking 'bout back home and that. I telling them 'bout saltfish. You know saltfish?"

I nodded.

The others looked on sceptically.

"They telling me that saltfish over here taste the same as back 'ome. I can't agree with that. What you think?"

I told him that because I'd left Jamaica at a young age I couldn't say.

"Oh, I see," he said, disappointed. "So you can't really talk 'bout saltfish with any authority. Shame. Shame."

I knew two things about salted cod: cooked with a vegetable, Ackee, it is Jamaica's national dish; and in the 1970s Jamaica's socialist government banned its importation to save foreign currency and because it has no nutritional value. It wasn't a popular measure and contributed to the government's downfall. But I thought it undiplomatic to volunteer such information to a middle-aged Barbadian reminiscing about the good things he'd left behind in the Caribbean.

Ron, the saltfish puritan, had lived in Liverpool for over thirty years. He had a loud voice, and a sort of devil-may-care attitude which I attributed to a mixture of old age and relative success. He gave talks to Merseyside police recruits on community relations. Ron had little respect for Liverpool-born blacks. He contemptuously dismissed them as lacking in ambition, lazy. "Some of them wouldn't even cross the road for a job," he insisted. That Liverpool had one of the highest levels of unemployment in Britain didn't matter. Since arriving from Barbados, he hadn't been a day without work.

"Mind you," he said after a moment's reflection, interrupting what had appeared like a thoughtless tirade, "though I ain't experience it personally, this here is a racist town. Is Liverpool invent racism."

Suddenly, the vehemence he had heaped on Liverpool-born blacks was directed against the city. "I tell them that all the time. They don't like it. But somebody has to tell them."

Eustace said he had no personal experience of racism, but agreed with Ron wholeheartedly. He recalled that a famous West Indian cricketer had once asked him why, despite the long presence of black people in Liverpool, neither of the city's football clubs had any black players. "I is a cricket man, meself," said Eustace, "so I didn't really think I could answer him. But later I think 'bout it and I realise that man was making a very serious point."

Slim, who sat in the far corner, had become noticeably excited at the mention of football. Though seated, he was obviously very tall, and had a long, narrow face with a high forehead and low, cropped hair which seemed to have received fastidious attention, despite its sparseness.

Eustace wanted to continue, but Slim interrupted him. "I could've told you that, man," he said passionately. "Every black person in Liverpool know that them clubs don't want no black people."

According to Slim, back in the Seventies the then Liverpool Football Club manager discovered an exciting local black player. The boy was compared to the legendary Pele. But he never played a first team home match for the club. Instead, he played in a few European games, and scored. The manager was discouraged from playing him at

Anfield, the club's stadium, by management and fans. Eventually he was sold to a West Midlands club.

Slim ended by saying to Ron in a conciliatory voice: "You know I don't agree with you on this saltfish t'ing. But on Liverpool and racism ah must agree with you one hundred per cent." He was younger than the others. Which was probably why he disagreed on saltfish memory and spoke with such authority on football.

Football is not just a game in Liverpool. It's more like a religion, dividing families, determining friendships, arousing fierce loyalties. It celebrates, reaffirms and asserts a community's identity. Attending a club match is comparable to the totemic rituals of primitive societies. Indeed, the violent behaviour of some football fans has been compared to that of marauding savage tribes.

Liverpool has two clubs – Everton and Liverpool. Seldom a football season passes without one of them winning a major trophy. And the clubs' colours – blue and white, and white and red respectively – are both feared and respected throughout the country. Despite an incident in which Liverpool football fans contributed to causing the death of 48 opposing fans in Belgium in 1985, the city remains proud of its clubs.

That black Liverpudlians felt excluded from the game spoke volumes about their relationship to the city. Not only were they a mere sub-plot in its history, they were also spectators in its most important collective ritual. Not participants.

The rum bottle was circulated, and we moved on to talking about politics. Ron lamented the shortage of black spokespersons in Britain. More people who spoke their minds – like him? – he argued was "the only way to stop these people walking over us." He exhausted himself in a tirade against

Liverpool's politicians and administrators. "I tell them that every day," he said, frustrated, angry and tired.

Eustace was far calmer. He expressed admiration for Bernie Grant, who, as a London councillor (now an MP) had incurred the press's wrath over the 1985 Broadwater Farm riots. Grant had said "the police got a bloody good hiding".

"I respect that man," said Eustace. "But, you know, he should learn a thing or two from the Englishman about diplomacy. Could've said the same things in different words. But I can tell you a lot of black people agree with him."

Ron then produced a diary embossed with the Merseyside Police badge. He had an appointment and had to leave. He wished me luck and departed, leaving a cloud of cigar smoke in his wake. With Ron's departure, Neville, a Guyanese, became more talkative. He had said very little in Ron's presence, as if overwhelmed by him. He spoke softly, with a slight Guyanese accent. I learnt that he had served in the RAF in the Second World War. Ground maintenance staff. He settled in Liverpool because its slow pace was closest to Georgetown, Guyana's capital.

Eustace revealed that the Caribbean Cultural Centre was going through difficult times. Not only was it underfunded, it was frequently criticised for being divorced from the surrounding neighbourhood. Black Liverpudlians found most of its activities irrelevant. A group of youngsters had occupied it the previous year, protesting at its failure to meet their needs. It was a problem of generation and culture. Most of the Centre's users, and all its members, were middle-aged Afro-Caribbeans. They came mainly from Barbados, Trinidad, Jamaica, Guyana, Dominica and St Lucia. Barbadians predominated. And the building echoed with the sound of dominoes almost every night.

The Centre's difficulties was one expression of a division

between post-war, Afro-Caribbean immigrants and black Liverpudlians. The latter had little or no connection with the Caribbean. Their fathers, grandfathers and great-grand-fathers were mostly African seamen, their mothers local women. But it wasn't a new division. The seamen themselves were never united to the point where they socialised together. They were divided by language. And each language group met in their own private clubs. These clubs still exist, bearing names like the Ibo Club, the Sierra Leone Club, the Yoruba Club, and the Somali Club. The Afro-Caribbean frequented them all, but belonged to none.

But Eustace, who was turning out to be a lay historian and sociologist, stressed that unity was always achieved when it mattered. As a new arrival in Liverpool in the early Sixties, he witnessed it himself. One night a pub frequented by black men and their white female friends was attacked by whites. Apparently such incidents were common. The police were called in to separate the warring sides. News of the fight quickly spread around Liverpool 8, and many black men made their way to the scene. One was Jimmy-the-Somali, a local character renowned for his shortness and excessive drinking. When Jimmy-the-Somali arrived the two sides, separated by the police, seemed determined to continue the battle. Drunk as usual, a bottle of whisky in his hand, he walked into the no-man's-land and loudly declared: "Be-cause my black brothers are in a fight and I'm black too, I will fight to the death with them if necessary." The contrast between Jimmy's dwarfish stature and his forceful pledge of solidarity was so great that everybody broke into laughter. The tension was dissipated and the men went their separate ways. Today Jimmy-the-Somali would probably have been charged with threatening behaviour.

Eustace and his companions couldn't direct me to the

person who had painted the street signs red, gold and green. But they told me his name, Leroy Cooper, and that he was a poet. They suggested I tried around Granby Street. In particular I should ask for Gaddafi.

Liverpool was in the firm grip of a white, icy calm next morning. It had snowed overnight and, to my relief, the temperature had risen. The sight of snow-covered roofs, trees and cars gave me a momentary child-like thrill. I drank my coffee recalling the enchantment of my first snowfall, a month from Jamaica, many years ago.

I entered Toxteth by a new route. It took me through newly built council houses and flats. Not even the blanket of fresh snow could beautify this gloomy, dark area. Many young trees had been uprooted. Their frozen branches and roots protruded through the snow. Whole blocks of flats were boarded up, overshadowing burnt-out houses. Here and there mongrel dogs rummaged for food amongst piles of rubbish which seemed to be on every street corner. That these houses and flats were less than five years old made it all the more depressing. Built after the 1981 riots, they were part of an effort to improve the inner city. But the ghetto refused to die, driving its occupants to destructive acts of arson and vandalism. The fires, I learned, were started by occupants who wanted to be rehoused, away from Toxteth.

The new housing continued into Granby Street, the heart of Liverpool 8. Wide and spacious, Granby Street, with its exotically named grocery stores, seemed incongruent with its surroundings. But that initial impression soon wore off as I went further along it. Half-way down Granby Street is a small plot of wasteland. As yet untouched by the developers, it's a dumping ground for broken furniture, car parts and the ubiquitous black plastic bags. A wall behind it serves as a sort of unofficial community noticeboard. Its most prominent message read: "This is Toxteth (sensimilla). Not Croxteth (Heroin)." It's a warning to heroin pushers against plying their deadly wares in the neighbourhood. Only ganja is acceptable.

Finding Gaddafi was easy. I asked a group of teenagers milling about outside a café. Their complexions ranged from very dark to almost white, and the majority were of mixed race. That it was bitterly cold – the temperature had fallen again – didn't seem to bother them. Protected by heavy denim jackets, they laughed and chattered like schoolboys. Some were probably of school age, but their serious, hard faces disguised that fact.

They all seemed to know Gaddafi and directed me to his base. One even accompanied me there. It wasn't far, and as we walked I asked him how he could stand outside in such weather. He shrugged his shoulders and said: "Better than lying in bed all day. Anyway, I'm working." After he left, I realised what he meant: he was selling ganja.

Gaddafi was the leader of a group known as the Frontline Posse. Tall and powerfully built, he had an easy laugh and exuded charisma. The name Gaddafi was apt. He wore a battle-green fatigue-uniform, a huge leather cap, with a single dreadlock hanging out, and a red Palestinian scarf, the type favoured by travelled left-wingers. But I suspected Gaddafi had little in common with the devotees of radical chic. He'd acquired his nickname in the 1981 Toxteth riots. The police had singled him out as a leader and he'd spent a year in jail as a result. After his release his friends began calling him Gaddafi. Like his Libyan namesake, Gaddafi lived on a frontline. Ironically, Gaddafi's father was a senior police officer in Barbados.

Gaddafi and the Frontline Posse were busy renovating a building they hoped would become a venue for the area's

Rasta brethren. They had previously managed a café and its success encouraged them to find larger premises. He showed me around. Upstairs was a bar with Mexican-style windows, polished floorboards and wood-panelled walls. Behind the bar were three framed pictures of Bob Marley, Haile Selassie and Marcus Garvey, the Rasta trinity.

Gaddafi looked long and hard at the Garvey picture and said:

"It's only at the age of thirty that I-man beginning to understand what Garvey stands for. Pride of the black man. You can't have pride if you always begging."

The entire refurbishment, Gaddafi stressed, was being done without any outside help. "We doing a independent t'ing. I-and-I didn't want no government handouts. Too many strings attached. And I-and-I don't want no Babylonian telling I-and-I what to do. Seen Rasta?"

Gaddafi had a habit of lapsing into Rasta-talk when he was saying, or thought he was saying, something radical. His days of rioting were over. He'd learnt from the 1981 uprisings "that them kind of things don't lead anywhere. A whole lot of people just get their heads busted. The police can go home to their nice suburban home. But we have to live in the ruins of Babylon. So we're trying to do something constructive. I-and-I not dealing with destruction. Seen Rasta?"

After the tour I was introduced to several members of the Frontline Posse. They were taking a break and sat huddled around a single-bar electric fire.

Robbie was the most talkative. Small, with a weasel-like face and wry smile, his facial features gave no clues as to his racial mixture. His mother turned out to be English, but he could not say about his father. "The man's a bastard," Robbie told me. He didn't know his father and his mother refused to speak about him. "Only a bastard brings a kid into the world then pisses off," he said, angry but still smiling.

As I sat talking Jonah came to join us. He was tall and had a narrow, gaunt face, topped by a woollen hat that looked like a beehive. Originally from Manchester, his father was Jamaican, his mother English. This mixture gave him a rich, golden-brown complexion. Jonah was in a foul mood and I later learnt why. Some days before, a vanload of young policemen had verbally abused him. Although he was alone, he warned them off. But the incident plagued him. So that morning he'd been to the local police station to register a complaint. He'd warned the desk officer to control his men or he, Jonah, would deal with them himself. "Told him I'd rip them apart with me bare hands," he said in a low, calm voice. With his huge calloused hands, it was a threat he seemed more than capable of carrying out.

The Frontline Posse, some of whom were the children of immigrants, others fifth- and sixth-generation Liverpudlians, seldom ventured outside Toxteth. For them, the rest of Liverpool was a hostile, unwelcoming place. The city-centre shops regarded them with suspicion. Store detectives invariably saw them as potential shoplifters. And it wasn't simply because they were Rastas. One Frontline Posse member, Selassie, who resembled his namesake, asked if I'd spent any time in the city centre and how many black people I'd seen there. I said I had but couldn't recall seeing many.

Selassie suggested that black Liverpudlians only went to the city centre out of necessity. He compared Liverpool to South Africa. "They don't call it apartheid," he said, "but it is in a way."

Liverpool's all-white football teams were again condemned.

And this time with angrier passion than I'd heard the day before. After football came Liverpool's no-go areas. Vicky, the girl in the pub, had mentioned the North End. I now heard it as solemn advice. Gaddafi warned me never to be caught in the North End after dark. A white working-class area, its inhabitants had a reputation for attacking black people.

At this point Gaddafi stood up and said in a voice laden with emotion: "Remember, this was THE slave port once. This city was built on our blood, our bones, our flesh. These people haven't changed since the days they used to pack us into ships like sardines or like dead meat. Seen Rasta?"

They all murmured in agreement. And Gaddafi proceeded to reel off a list of famous Liverpool names associated with the slave trade. I now understood why he was the leader of the Frontline Posse.

I spent many hours with the Frontline Posse. A few would drift off to work, then return to join the discussion. And visitors regularly passed by, some just to say hello, others to talk for a while. Not all were black either. Two white guys who dropped in were greeted with the same warmth and friendliness as the other visitors. One, Martin, had been to school with Gaddafi. When Gaddafi joked that Martin was now spending all his time in the North End, he, Martin, explained why they hadn't seen him for a while. He'd been working in a factory for a month. But the owner refused to heat the place. So he'd given up the job.

Selassie scoffed and remarked that he would have brought in his own heating. But Gaddafi went even further and said: "More time still, you wouldn't catch me dead working in no factory."

Martin's presence surprised me and, after he'd left, I remarked on it to Selassie. A white guy in their company seemed odd, considering our earlier conversation. Selassie's reply was direct and honest: "He's from round here so he's all right. Guys like that check for us and we check for them. You know, peace and love." He went on to explain that there was no hostility between black and white in Toxteth. The area was too mixed up for that.

Some time later we were joined by yet another visitor, a startlingly skinny young man by the name of Asha. In spite of the cold, Asha wore no socks, only espadrilles, thin cotton trousers and a cardigan over a T-shirt. He sat for a long while without speaking, but chain-smoked roll-up cigarettes. His hands trembled constantly, giving the impression that he suffered from some nervous disorder.

Selassie's remark that visiting Africa was his greatest ambition – his grandfather was Liberian – seemed to awaken Asha, who leaned forward in his chair and said, grinning stupidly, "I've been to Africa."

I looked at him in surprise.

"He's a seaboy, that one," said Selassie.

"It's the motherland, mon," Asha said. He spoke with a curious mixture of Liverpudlian and West African pidgin English.

"Where in Africa?" I asked.

"Lagos, Accra, Freetown. One day me will go back for good."

"But you were born in Liverpool?"

"Yeah, me born here. But me is not a Liverpudlian. Me come from the homelands, mon. Africa."

I too had been to Lagos and asked what he thought of the Nigerian capital.

"Is me home, mon. Me father is from there. But is rough, you know. A lot of hustling in Lagos. Mean city, mon."

When I asked why he wasn't at sea he told me this story. The son of a Nigerian sailor and a local white woman, Asha had three years before worked on a Shell ship. On his last voyage the first mate was a white South African. As soon as the ship left port, the first mate seized every opportunity to harass and racially abuse Asha. He tolerated it for a few days then reported the matter to the captain. The captain promised to speak to the first mate. But a week later, the first mate's abuses of "Nigger" and "Kaffir" had still not ceased. So Asha decided to deal with his tormentor. One day, as the first mate was going through a fire door, Asha slammed it on him. Its weight sent the first mate crashing to the floor and Asha laid into him, kicking him until he was unconscious. "Right, I've had enough of you," Asha said to the bloody figure. The incident cost him his job. He was sent back to Liverpool at the next port. An industrial tribunal exonerated him, but the Seamen's Union suspended him for three years. Asha's suspension was now nearing its end. But as I watched his shaky hand light and relight his cigarettes, his face as gaunt as a malnourished child's, I doubted that he would ever return to sea. A wreck kept afloat by an illusion that sea life, normality for him, awaited the end of his punishment.

Nothing I'd seen or heard in Liverpool touched me as much as Asha's story: not the city's shameful past, because that is unchangeable; to contemplate otherwise is to risk a potentially destructive self-torture; not the Frontline Posse's description of Liverpool's black life – they were surviving it. But it was destroying Asha, that fragile, almost ghostly figure, momentarily victorious in defending his dignity, but ultimately defeated.

Gaddafi and his friends couldn't help in my search for the Liverpool poet and sign painter. The Frontline Posse leader described him as "the kind of guy you see everyday for a week then you don't see him again for ages". And nobody knew where Leroy Cooper lived. If he came by, they promised to let him know I wanted to meet him.

As I made to leave, Asha spoke again: "You want to know about Liverpool?" he asked, nervous and uncertain.

"Yes."

"Then talk to the old seamen. They'll tell you all about Liverpool." He looked away, as if withdrawing to whatever distant region of his mind made him such a silent, haunted figure, and repeated: "Talk to the old seamen."

Many of Vince's drinking and domino-playing companions were former sailors. From these friends, he found me two old men of the sea and accompanied me to see the first, a Sierra Leonean by the name of Holy Joe. Without Vince as an interpreter, much of what Holy Joe had to say would have been lost. Although Holy Joe had been in Britain since 1916, he still spoke in Creole, particularly when talking about the past.

Holy Joe lived in an old people's home in Toxteth. It was the final resting place of a man who, from his own account, had lived a long and remarkable life. He claimed to be 108 years old, but had the physical appearance and mental agility of a much younger man. Old tars are notorious for their tall tales, so much of what Holy Joe said had to be taken with a pinch of salt, Vince advised me. He provided a clue to the veracity of his stories by quoting a West African maxim: "form fool, to get wisdom."

Holy Joe Johnson was just one of the many African sailors attracted to Liverpool during its heyday. Exactly how he got there wasn't clear, but within days of arriving he secured a job on a British warship. Unfortunately, the night before it was due to leave port, Holy Joe was beaten unconscious and robbed. When he woke up his newly bought shoes and trousers and all his money had been stolen. A good samaritan, a Liberian, sheltered and nursed him until he was well again. When Holy Joe went to the docks to enquire about his ship, he learnt that it had been sunk by a U-boat.

That was the first of his miraculous escapes from death. Others happened in the Second World War. His most memorable one occurred when he was hired as head cook in a new battleship. He took the job reluctantly. Two previous cooks had been dismissed for excessive drinking, and Joe, a teetotaller, was recommended. With nine cooks, all white, in his charge he had never held such a responsible post. His fears that they wouldn't obey his orders soon proved groundless. It was the navy and they were bound to follow his command. Joe worked on the ship for over a week while it was still in port. Some time in the second week he was taking a rest when he was woken by the spirit of his dead father. The spirit ordered him not to sail with the ship, otherwise he would never return alive. He protested that he had little choice. He had received a substantial advance payment. The spirit insisted, "You not going on that ship. You and me, which one is first?"

"You, sir," Hoiy Joe replied, humbly.

His father's spirit reassured him that the advanced wages he'd received posed no problems. "Everything will come to pass," the spirit said.

The next afternoon, as Joe was working in the galley, the river began to swell. It caused the ship to roll violently. Several objects in the galley were dislodged. A pot of hot oil fell on Holy Joe's foot, burning him badly. The ship's doctor examined Holy Joe and sent him to hospital. There another doctor bandaged the foot and recommended that Holy Joe go home. A visiting nurse called twice a day. Meanwhile, the battleship had to sail without Holy Joe. Just beyond Holyhead, it was attacked by a German destroyer. "Not a soul survived," said Holy Joe. "Three hundred and fifty men went down, down."

Holy Joe claimed that the spirits of his parents saved him on numerous occasions from certain death. And for this reason, he was a devout Christian. His godfearing ways, he believed, were responsible for his long life. But it was not always advantageous. One landlord, another Sierra Leonean, once interrogated him about his leisure activities before refusing him a room.

"You smoke?" the landlord asked.

"No sir," Holy Joe replied.

"You go with women?"

"No sir."

"You gamble?"

"No sir."

Clearly annoyed, the landlord said, "Then how ah go make money from you? No room."

Holy Joe later became a landlord himself, owning nine houses and a nightclub. The houses were acquired through his first wife, a white woman, because the vendors wouldn't sell to him. "When me go for house, they say they na go give for niggers."

His late second wife had been a widow and a doctor. Recalling her, Holy Joe's face assumed a blissful expression. For a moment he seemed lost in some happy memory which he couldn't share with us. Then he snapped out of it and said: "That woman, na good woman. English women, if they love you, they go kill dey brother and dey father for you. If they no love you, you nah bastard."

He looked across the room to a large Edwardian sideboard. On top of it were photographs of Holy Joe's numerous children. Some, he explained, were in the United States, some in Sierra Leone, and a few in Britain. One of his sons still lived in Liverpool and regularly visited. Another picture showed top-hatted Holy Joe meeting the Queen. But pride of place went to a black-and-white portrait of Mrs Thatcher. "She," Holy Joe declared, "dat woman. She de one woman ah want to marry before I go die."

Over a week away in this depressed northern city, Holy Joe was the first Thatcher admirer I'd met. I pressed him to explain what he found attractive about the Prime Minister. But he wouldn't say anything more than "Dat woman, dey strong-o".

Holy Joe's conversation remained in this lighthearted vein throughout. He was obviously delighted to have visitors on that cold, January night. We were an audience for his humour and wit. But as we neared the end, with Holy Joe visibly tiring, he called us closer to him. We complied and he tapped the back of his wrinkled, leathery hand and said: "See this colour. Nobody like this colour. You know why?"

We shook our heads.

"Because the world rob we. They take everything from us. They scatter my people all over the world. But one day, they go back in Africa. One day."

Then he slumped in his chair. He had probably spoken more in two hours than in the entire past week.

I was surprised at Holy Joe's final observation. For almost two hours he'd recalled his life with much good humour and not without the sense of mischief with which he'd probably lived it. Yet his last words could have issued from the lips of a 1960s' Black Nationalist, or a Rasta.

Nonetheless, I felt somewhat disappointed with Holy Joe. I felt that little he'd said justified Asha's insistence that the "old seamen" could help in my understanding of Liverpool 8.

A Liverpool University lecturer, Tony Lane, made me aware of the next seaman I met. Lane, an outsider to Liverpool, had carried out research into Liverpool seafarers. One of his conclusions stressed the casual and therefore uncertain nature of employment in the docks. Black sailors were particularly insecure. They were employed according to the economic cycle, even those born in Liverpool. As with other forms of employment, the shipping lines always gave jobs to whites first.

In the course of his research Lane had spoken to many sailors, black and white. Not all had been forthcoming. One seaman who had refused to talk was Ludwig Hesse, whom Lane described as a Jamaican. A former community activist, Hesse was said to have locked the world out over the past few years. I'd never once met a Jamaican who didn't welcome a fellow Jamaican. So I decided to try my luck. Hesse's name was in the telephone directory. Rather than telephone, I went to call on him one afternoon. He lived in a council block overlooking a park. A dark, frail and dignified-looking old man answered the door. In stating the purpose of my call, I slipped in the fact that I was a Jamaican. He was un-impressed.

"I don't give interviews to anybody," he said, grim-faced and suspicious.

"Why not?" I asked, my mind working furiously to find some way of preventing him from closing the door. One thing was clear from the few words he'd spoken: he wasn't a Jamaican.

"Too much rubbish has been written about Liverpool 8. And lies, lies."

"I'm looking for the truth," I said, trying flattery, "and I've been told you're the best person to talk to." He'd been about to close the door but he hesitated and I carried on at a frantic pace. "I was told that you came from Jamaica before the war and . . ."

"Young man," he interjected. "My wife was a Jamaican, and some of my closest friends have been Jamaicans. But I come from Ghana."

"Oh, sorry. I was misinformed. So you're Kwame Nkrumah's countryman."

At the mention of the late Ghanaian leader's name his face relaxed. "Yes, yes," he said. "What do you know about Nkrumah?"

"Oh, I lived in Nigeria for a while and travelled to Ghana by road once."

He now looked at me with curiosity. I thought he would invite me in, but instead he said: "Look it's very cold and I have an hospital appointment. Give me your number and I'll call you. Maybe I'll have some time the day after next."

I gave him my telephone number and walked away feeling unsure whether I'd hear from him. Two days later, as I prepared to go out, Ludwig Hesse called. He would see me that afternoon.

Ludwig Hesse's living-room had an elegant sparseness to it. The velvet-covered three-piece suite looked almost brand-new, and was arranged to face the colour television. It wasn't at all the kind of room you'd associate with a former sailor.

He offered me a drink, whisky. Then he gently lowered himself into an armchair. I tried to guess his age, but there was something ageless about his dark, unblemished face. We drank a toast, and he sighed and said: "Young man, if you're going to go knocking on people's doors, you must forget about us all being black. You could have been a conman."

I interpreted this remark both as sound advice, and an oblique apology for his earlier unfriendliness.

I gathered that Ludwig Hesse had lived in Liverpool since before the Second World War. He came from Christenberg in Ghana. Now the seat of Ghana's government, it was named after King Christian IV of Denmark. His Germanic name, he assured me, is quite common in that part of Ghana. "I've got German blood in me," he said with more than a little pride. Indeed, Ludwig Hesse had much to be proud of. He'd sailed on the first British ship to leave Reykjavik in the Second World War. Shortly after the war, he left the sea, and worked as an electrician and got involved in community politics. Now he was dying. Cancer. His life consisted of regular hospital visits and endless operations. Illness and old age caused his thoughts to wander, and he seemed unable to dwell on one theme for too long. But in his lucid moments, he revealed an acute political awareness.

Politically, he belonged to the Black Consciousness tradition. The late Steve Biko was, said Hesse, the most recently famous bearer of that tradition. In the past, he'd worked with many notable black political figures. He recalled Paul Robeson with fondness, often referring to the Afro-American actor and singer by his first name. Dr Hastings Banda, now Malawi's President, was another former comrade. "A different man, then," he said. Banda used to run a surgery in Toxteth in the Forties.

Hesse's early political activities involved organising street-corner rallies in Liverpool 8. The message of those rallies stressed the unity between the struggles of Afro-Americans, Afro-Caribbeans, and Africans. But it wasn't easy in a community of sailors: "You had blacks who used to say, 'Oh, man I'm going home. As soon as I get a bit of money, man, I'm going home.'"

But there were enough black political activists to get things done. They got involved in issues outside Britain, too.

Once responding to a famous rape case in the United States, Ludwig and his comrades organised a petition. A delegation comprising both black and white travelled down to London, to the US embassy. A black man was to present the petition. But they were kept waiting a long time by the American counsellor. When they were finally admitted, the counsellor refused to acknowledge Hesse as the delegation leader. A white member of the delegation, speaking in the haughtiest imperial tones, stepped forward and addressed the counsellor thus: "I must remind you, sir, that you're on His Majesty's territory. This isn't the US. So you are required to show courtesy to His Majesty's subjects."

Hesse's white political comrades generally included left-wingers. But he believed that many white socialists are tainted with "a fear of the black man". He recalled addressing a trade union meeting in the Forties. During question-time a white member of the audience got up and said: "Sir, when I was a boy my father used to say 'Always keep the black man down. Never let him rise above you, because if he does, he'll take revenge for all the wrongs we've done him in the past.'"

"I could not help but smile," Hesse said to me. "I told him that his father had taught him nonsense. Because if the black man was in a position of strength to take revenge, at least half of Europe would have to be destroyed. He understood me. Many of us had fought in the war together. The blood. The killing. Nobody wanted to see that again."

Most of Hesse's political activities were focused on Liverpool. It was, he said, an immigrant city, but white Liverpudlians were reluctant to accept that fact. And their general attitude to black Liverpudlians never ceased to amaze him. "When more black people began settling here after the war, you'd have thought that Liverpool would be

47

the first place to have started some kind of community relations council. But we had to fight tooth and nail for one. We got it only after a mass meeting in the town hall.

"Liverpool's history of racism is unending. They even have the cheek, the city fathers, to think there has never been a slave trade."

With his long history of political involvement, Hesse was, perhaps understandably, annoyed with the younger generation of blacks who criticised his generation. "They say we never fought back," he said bitterly. "But we were fighting back from day one. The accomoos in Ghana hoisted the red flag way before they knew anything about Marxism."

I said that it seemed to me that part of being black involved an endless struggle. And sometimes I wasn't sure what was being fought for or against.

"Equal rights," he replied sharply. "That's all. You have to understand that racism is embedded in these people's mind. It won't be removed easily. We will get as far as we're able to. We will get equal rights. But to say that we're going to be embraced as brothers and sisters, God will have to do that one."

Many years had passed since Ludwig Hesse's political days. But he was a close follower of the British political and social scene. Black people's future was his primary concern. The violent events of 1981 had most surprised him: "I didn't have any regrets about what took place in 1981. Equally before '81. The Bristol incident. When I heard about Bristol and then saw what happened in Liverpool, I said to myself, what a coincidence. Two former slaving ports. The great-great-grandchildren have come here to take revenge. Of course lives were lost. But you know how many of our people were dumped in the sea. God works in mysterious ways."

"So you do believe in revenge," I said.

"No," he replied firmly. "Revenge will get us nowhere. It prolongs the battle. I've seen enough killing and dying in my times. I don't care for more. But for years and years we talked and we talked to these people. Did they listen? No. Now they have to, though. Or see their cities destroyed. But the coincidence, Liverpool and Bristol. You couldn't help but notice it."

I knew of no connection between Ludwig Hesse and the Frontline Posse. Yet he articulated the same sentiments as theirs, but more forcefully and with greater eloquence. The Frontline Posse had left me with the impression that Liverpool was a city haunted by its past. And Ludwig Hesse, with his long residence here, and the authority that came with age, had confirmed it.

Some days later, I happened to be talking to a group of white Christians. They ran a bookshop and small church hall on Granby Street. Toxteth, their leader Euan argued, was a spiritual wasteland. Material improvements of the area weren't enough. People here needed Christianity. Like everybody else I'd met in Liverpool, they stressed that the riots of '81 and '85 were not race riots. The entire community had reacted against policing practices which were more suited to an occupied territory, or a colony, like northern Ireland. These were the observations of socially concerned, committed Christians. Some had obviously given up comfortable suburban lifestyles to practise their faith in the inner city.

They did make one remark that astonished me. A schoolteacher, a southerner who had lived in Liverpool for fifteen years, said: "Back in the '81, the spiritual legacy of how Liverpool became great, i.e. on the slave trade, played a part. Wealth from the slave trade built the city, the parks and what-have-you. Granby Street is named after *The Marquis of*

Granby, one of the first slave ships. People know that. During the '81 riots a statue of Huskisson was pulled down because he was a slaver.

"There's a spiritual legacy. You know, it says in the Bible that the sins of the fathers will be visited on to the sons of the third and fourth generation. People may write that off as being a bit old-fashioned. But in terms of spiritual cause and effect, if you build a city on slave trading, then you maintain the economic gap between the two races after slavery. I think conflict is inevitable. Though not an immediate cause, Liverpool's past is contributing to its present troubles."

The Frontline Posse, Ludwig Hesse, and now a group of white Christians. It seemed that whoever I spoke to pointed me in the same direction. Liverpool would not be allowed to forget its past. The people of Toxteth would see to that.

The Municipal Building in Dale Street reflected Liverpool's general decay. Its dirt-encrusted, crumbling façade was matched by ancient corridors of gritty floors, flaking wall-paint, collapsing ceilings and stone steps worn down to a dangerous smoothness. Its workers moved with the lethargic grace of bureaucrats in a corruption-riddled, post-colonial bureaucracy in some tropical country. Only the chill breeze coming through broken windows and the white faces reminded me that I was in England.

A ruddy-faced commissioner directed me to the second floor. There I stopped outside the office where I had an appointment. The only door with a spyhole, its surface was pockmarked with indentations. The type produced by violent kicks. I knocked, waited, but got no reply.

I was there to meet Sampson Bond. A Tanzanian sailor had sung Bond's praises, and insisted we met. The sailor had ignored my indifference to the prospect of such a meeting and telephoned him in my presence, leaving me with little choice but to arrange an appointment. I began to write a note to Bond, to show that I'd been there. Sampson Bond was Liverpool's Principal Race Relations Adviser. The post was created after many decades of bitter argument between Liverpool 8's black leaders and the city council. It was to be the first step in improving relations between an alienated community and a distant local government administration that had determinedly ignored the city's black population.

But the Toxteth people had declared Sampson Bond the wrong man for the job. He was an outsider, a Londoner with no experience of Liverpool, or the intricacies of race relations work. They refused to co-operate with him and chose every opportunity virulently to denounce the foreigner. One slogan played on their slave past: "No more Bondage". And threats of physical violence were used to deter Bond from entering Liverpool 8. Yet Bond was there. Why?

He arrived before I finished the note. I'd expected an older person, but he was young, casually dressed, and walked with the bounce of an athlete. He apologised for being late. He'd just returned from London. I should have received a message that he might be a little late. We decided to have lunch and he led the way. A picket line had formed outside the Municipal Building. What they were protesting about was unclear. Some of the picketers looked at us as we passed by. Whispers of Sam Bond's name spread amongst them. But they seemed uncertain which of us was the villain.

"Nalgo workers," Bond said, once we'd passed the protesters.

"What is it about?" I asked.

"Some dispute with the council," he said vaguely. "They don't like me either. The Union's instructed its members not to work with me."

"On what grounds?"

"Sympathy with local blacks. But it's a con. They're really trying to protect their jobs. Did you see any black people there?"

The picket line had been all white.

We ate in a bar-cum-bistro. Throughout the meal, Bond was greeted by other customers. But their greetings were always from a distance, and their smiles more sympathetic than friendly. I learned that Bond was born in Guyana and brought to England as a child. On graduation from a polytechnic as a surveyor, he almost went to work in Trinidad. "The racism in Britain," he said, "made it an attractive option. I just wanted to get out." But the job fell through. So he worked for a London council, whose equal opportunities policies were opening doors for black graduates like himself. But the work was monotonous. In the evenings, after work, Sam Bond canvassed for the Labour Party and attended meetings. Politicking gave him more satisfaction than the building department where he worked. It was more "meaningful". The Liverpool job offered a chance to earn a living from what he most enjoyed. He seized the opportunity. He considered his inexperience irrelevant. After all, "race relations work is only a few years old".

Liverpool, he confessed, was a frustrating and disappointing experience. He'd been physically attacked in his office. His assailants had been "hired thugs". He had some sympathisers in Toxteth, especially the post-war Afro-Caribbean immigrants. They advised him to call in the police. But he couldn't bring himself to do that.

"I don't understand these people," Bond said, incredulous, pained. "They complain that the Town Hall doesn't employ them. That it does nothing for them. I'm there to create jobs. I could create three hundred jobs tomorrow. But they won't give me a chance." His gaze was unwavering, like a man utterly convinced of his rightness. The flames of zealotry blazed in his eyes.

"They've been here for centuries," I said. "Maybe they feel insulted that an outsider should be preferred to a local candidate. It's an important job, the city's first Race Relations Adviser."

"Their problem isn't going to be solved just by better race relations," Bond said. "People have to be mobilised. The system has to be destroyed. That's the only cure for racism."

"Black and white unity in Liverpool? I've never seen a more racially divided city."

"That comes from centuries of racism. I know all about the North End. I only go there with white escorts. But we've got to overcome that. People have got to recognise that the system that enslaved us is the same system that oppresses whites and feeds them with racist ideas. Most black people in Liverpool are blind to that."

"Maybe they're not interested in destroying the system. Maybe they just want it to work more for their benefit. Acknowledge their right to an equal share of the cake."

"We're trying to make that happen for both blacks and whites. But some people in Toxteth are determined to prevent it. Last year I was invited to address a meeting there. They wouldn't let me speak." He sounded genuinely hurt.

We were going round in circles. Sam Bond seemed incapable of understanding the hostility he faced. Despite his fighting talk, his opponent had rendered him impotent. But his revolutionary zeal, fired by a crude Marxism, had made him susceptible. Dogma and an almost religious fervour had driven him into a lonely, friendless corner.

"What I don't understand", I said, "is why you don't simply leave. Find another job."

"Because not everybody is opposed to me. There's some hope. The administration up here is really trying to do something different. They've placed real change on the agenda."

Bond was referring to the Labour-controlled council which had employed him. The council leaders were members of Militant Tendency, which dominated the local Labour Party. Through the rose-tinted spectacles of militants the working-class is an homogeneous mass, equally exploited and oppressed by the capitalist system. All divisions within the working-class are created by the capitalists. To recognise those divisions is to perpetuate them. It was a classic case of confusing what is with what ought to be. Militant was a popular local government – but not with black Liverpudlians.

By ignoring the race factor, this most radical administration was prolonging the centuries-old invisibility of black Liverpudlians. The Race Relations Adviser post was a reluctant concession to the reality of race. A locally recruited race adviser would have been too race-conscious. So Militant brought in Sam Bond, a comrade who'd earned his political colours canvassing in London. The result was a war of attrition, the local government on one side, Toxteth blacks on the other, and Sam Bond in the middle.

Bond had given me the Party answer to why he should stay. Later on in our conversation he was more honest.

"I've been here for two years. I haven't been able to do anything. Everybody knows what's happening up here. It's been in all the newspapers. Who's going to give me a job after this?"

I couldn't answer him. On one level, he was a young man who'd made an ill-advised move in an effort to improve his career. He'd made an irreparable mistake. It was too late to retreat with honour. On another level, he was a blinkered ideologue whose unreal politics and stubbornness had led him up a cul-de-sac. (Six months later Labour was defeated in the local election. Bond was made redundant, but he was still insistent that Liverpool needed him.)

One afternoon I ate lunch in the Penny Lane Café. Beatles memorabilia decorated its walls – album sleeves, actual records, newspaper cuttings and autographed photographs of John, Paul, George and Ringo. It was a cosy, almost homely, shrine to the four Liverpool musicians who became the definitive symbols of a decade, the 1960s. The waitress was friendly and seemed as curious about me as I was about the décor. In this nostalgic ambience, I recalled a feature of my early years in London. I grew up around Ladbroke Grove and Portobello Road. Many houses in the neighbourhood were occupied by flower children, the peace-and-love generation. People with flowers in their hair and bells on their ankles were a common sight. So too, of course, were discarded syringes and pain-racked junkies. Even a child could tell that the garden of peace was being choked by deadly weeds. And for a long time the Beatles – especially John Lennon – and the flower children whom they personified, were inextricably associated in my mind.

Many years later, I was teaching in Nigeria when, with the rest of the world, I heard the news of John Lennon's death. It was as if someone I knew and respected had died. I remembered commenting to a Nigerian colleague about the tragic news. But he was untouched. Hippies and peace and love had never been a part of his childhood. A fellow Afro-Caribbean lecturer could share my sense of tragedy, though. He'd grown up in Canada.

That Christmas, 1980, Lennon's most famous song, "Imagine", was played at every expatriate party.

I left the Penny Lane Café humming the lyrics of "Imagine". And I was still humming it when I got on a bus for Toxteth. But the words stopped when I sat down. In front of me, on the back of a seat, scrawled in huge red letters, were the words: "Nigger go back to the jungle." It was a rude reminder that I was in Liverpool, not the utopia that Liverpool-born Lennon hauntingly wished for.

My destination was the office of a self-help group. My search for Leroy Cooper, the poet and sign-painter, had brought me here.

A Chinese man engrossed in a computer display was the only person in a small, shambolic office. Despite his initial reluctance he turned out to be very useful. The organisation's book contained the number of a Mr Cooper. I was allowed to use the office telephone. A gruff, Jamaican-accented voice answered at the other end. It belonged to Leroy Cooper's father. Unfortunately, Leroy Cooper didn't live with him. "Would you be interested in talking to me?" Mr Cooper asked after I'd explained why I was looking for his son. "I've had some nasty brushes with these people in Liverpool."

I was growing weary of listening to people's complaints, but agreed to meet him later that day. Meanwhile he would try to track down his son for me. As I put down the phone, two men entered the office. Their proprietorial air signalled that they were the bosses. One was short, dark and dressed in a sober business suit. The other was much younger, brown-skinned, and had cropped, receding gingerish hair and freckles.

"Hope that wasn't a long distance call," the older man, who resembled an elf, said.

"No, it was local," I said, and introduced myself. My mention of the media brought a swift, disapproving response.

"The media, eh," said the ginger-haired fellow, whose name was Steven Connors. "We got no time for the media in here."

"I was enquiring about someone. Leroy Cooper," I said.

"Oh, our poet." He sounded as if he was disappointed that I wasn't there to speak to him. But he smiled for the first time, revealing a mouth of many glittering gold-capped teeth.

I elaborated on why I was in Liverpool. He asked why I had chosen Liverpool and not, say, Manchester, another large northern city with a large black population. My answer came out quite thoughtlessly: "Firstly, it's the home of the Beatles . . ."

Steve interjected like a lion pouncing on its hapless victim: "The Beatles? We got no time for the Beatles round here. They're just another example of the white music industry ripping off black music. Where do you think the Beatles learnt their craft? They come from up Penny Lane way. There are no nightclubs up there. They learnt it round here, in Liverpool 8. John and Paul were taught to play the guitar by a Trinidadian guy, Woodvine. He used to own a nightclub that played Stateside music. He was a musician himself. John and Paul used to hang around him. That's where they picked up their style from. But nobody ever mentions Woodvine. Nobody! When Woodvine opened another night club he invited them to the opening. They didn't go, they were too big to know him then. So we round here don't have any time for the bloody Beatles."

This angry response, delivered in a thick Liverpudlian accent, was my second reminder of where I was. His ferocity startled me.

I told him I was unaware of the Beatles' Toxteth connection.

"That's the way they, white people, want it," said Shaun. "Scratch most white successes and you'll find an exploited black man below the surface."

Steve later calmed down. He invited me to stay a while. A boy, who had come in as we spoke, was sent to buy some tea and biscuits. Steve instructed the boy to avoid a certain shop because it stocked South African goods. "We've told them often enough, but they won't listen," he said. It was a display of radicalism intended as much for my benefit as for the little boy's street education.

Steve Connors was an archetypal angry young man. In the short time I spent in his company he expressed anger at the community in which he was born, at the city's all-white institutions, at the police and at the government. Even his parents weren't spared. He described his upbringing as "regretful" because his Nigerian father, an Ibo, like many African seamen, had failed to impart his culture. He had grown up knowing only his mother's culture. I'd heard similar sentiments from other black Liverpudlians. Clearly the sins of the fathers were not confined to white Liverpool.

When J. B. Priestley, on his famous English Journey, stopped in Liverpool, a class of "half-caste" children prompted him to ask: "Will some of them, after extraordinary adventures and vicissitudes, be found, hence . . . defying us in Africa, inspired by memories of England that do not extend beyond tenements and dark streets in a dock-side slum?"

Perhaps in Priestley's time "half-caste" Britons migrated to their father's home. Not any more. The docks no longer afford as many opportunities for adventures. The Liverpool-born mixed race person is stuck there. Intimately familiar with but rejected by his mother's culture he is the bearer of an immediate anger that lashes out in all directions.

The inner city riots that swept through Britain in the early Eighties were described as being particularly fierce in Liverpool 8. Perhaps the city's sordid history played a part. But undoubtedly, the racial composition of the community also contributed. In an environment of racial prejudice, the person of mixed race must experience it more acutely than others. He is not an immigrant. He has immediate blood ties with his rejectors. But unlike the children of immigrants, he cannot easily fall back on a culture that is exclusively his own. In the search for an understanding of his predicament there's always a danger that he will embrace an extreme racial nationalism that promotes hatred of his tormentors – whites. But this only leads to further confusion. His mother is white, a member of the oppressing group. To despise her is to despise himself.

Of course, not all mixed-race people travel this road of extreme confusion. Those that do must end up as psychiatric cases. The more moderate ones can, perhaps, become the most effective opponents of racial prejudice, because they are both a part of the racist culture and its victims.

Steve Connors showed dangerous tendencies towards racial nationalism. But he was not yet a full convert. I asked him how he felt about his mother. His answer was unequivocally favourable. That, in my eyes, was his one redeeming feature.

Mr Cooper senior lived outside Toxteth, near Wavertree Park, another working-class district. The taxi-driver who took me there was a garrulous, laughing fellow. Although middle-aged, he'd only been driving taxis for five years. Before that he worked in factories. When I told him that I lived in London, he was quick to volunteer his experience of the capital. He'd worked there for six months in the late Seventies.

"'Orrible place," he said. "Nobody talks to you. Nobody smiles. Lived for three months in a bedsit without once seeing another person in the house. And it was great big house."

"Is that why you came back to Liverpool?" I asked.

"Mainly. It's not easy up here. And that bloody government down in London doesn't make it easier. That Mrs Thatcher and her lot. 'Ave you seen our garden centre?"

"No."

"Great big thing it is. We had some riots up here. So Mrs Thatcher and her mob decides that what we need is bleeding flowers. Flowers! I ask you! I only give flowers when one of my relatives is sick. Tells you how they see us down there."

His laughter filled the cab, drowning the roar of the evening traffic. And I laughed with him, but reflected that the Thatcherite prognosis was a mockery, but, perhaps its diagnosis wasn't wide of the mark.

The speed with which Mr Cooper opened the door suggested that he'd been looking out for my arrival. He was a small, anxious man with a fretful, brown face. His speech was slow and was a mixture of Jamaican and Liverpudlian. We sat in an immaculately clean living-room. A poster of Bob Marley adorned one wall. On another was a colourful, erotic print of a black couple embracing.

Mr Cooper had not been able to contact his son, Leroy. "Is months me don't see him now," he said apologetically. "Me leave a message with 'im mother. 'Im go there quite a bit." He rang his ex-wife's number to find out if the message had been passed on. It hadn't. "And you know, I don't even know where that boy live," he said, putting down the phone. His brow knitted, as if he'd just made a weighty confession. His worried, grave expression belied his age. I learned later on that he was in his mid-forties.

From Mr Cooper I discovered that Leroy had played a central role in the 1981 riots. Leroy's attempt to prevent a policeman arresting a friend in Granby Street had sparked off the riots. He was jailed afterwards, and again some years later for reasons which Mr Cooper seemed uncertain about. Leroy's encounters with the law were now history. But Mr Cooper himself was embroiled in a long-running battle with the police. It began in 1979 when the police raided his house. A girl in his eldest son's school wrongly informed the police that there was stolen property to be found in Mr Cooper's house. "They brought three cars," he said, "and they kick down the door. Said they were looking for stolen property. They didn't find no stolen goods here. But they prosecute my lad. They took away my stuff. I had a bicycle for one of my lads, they took that and kept it for three months. A few days before my lad was due in court they came again. Said they were looking for stolen jewellery. They lock me up. When I was released I had to stand bail for my son."

The police returned a second time, Mr Cooper believed, because he had made an official complaint against them. His son's case was dismissed from court. But his complaint took rather longer. It had only just been concluded. He'd won, but had to pay two-thirds of the legal costs, which far outweighed his compensation. Meanwhile, his youngest son had also gotten in trouble with the police. Again Mr Cooper was convinced that his son had been wrongfully arrested. He intended to sue the police again.

"I know I can't win," said Mr Cooper, his face now a mask of anger and indignation, "You got your rights, but you can't beat the police. You win and you don't win. I still haven't got a penny for my door that was kicked in."

"If you know you can't win, why continue suing the police," I asked.

"I believe in my rights," he said firmly. "Anywhere I goes in this world, I'll fight for my rights. I'm a Jamaican. You can take me out of Jamaica, but you can't take Jamaica out of me."

He showed me a collection of newspaper cuttings on his eight-year battle with the police. Several national newspapers and magazines had reported his case. One notoriously rightwing daily had given him favourable coverage. Mr Cooper's Kafkaesque experience obsessed him. I tried to shift the conversation to his son, but again and again he would return to his persecution by the police. His speech alternated between calm appeals for some explanation of his ordeal, and a stubborn determination not to yield. He had earned the right to live in peace. For almost eighteen years he had worked at a local Ford plant. Redundancy caused him to leave. Since then he had worked for a packing company. He was a responsible man who after his divorce had started another family. All he wanted in life was respect for his rights. But the local police were as determined to make life uncomfortable for him, as he was to resist them.

Had he thought of leaving Britain, returning to Jamaica? "I'd like to go back one day," he told me. "But right now it'd be like leaving the frying-pan for the fire. I know this isn't my country but when I think about leaving my country in my youth days, coming to this country, and working for twenty-odd years, until I'm ready to go no one's going to drive me out.

"As far I'm concerned the white man robbed my fore-fathers and mash up my real country, I can't even go back to it, and build up their country. There's just no way I'm going to walk away."

I presumed that by his "real country" he meant Jamaica, though he could have meant Africa. I didn't get a chance to ask. He discovered a newspaper cutting which I hadn't seen and began to discuss that.

Most people keep newspaper cuttings of their triumphs. Mr Cooper's were of his unending nightmare. I was uncertain whether to admire or pity him. Perhaps he needed neither, just the vindication of a stranger, a fellow Jamaican a long way from home. I left him mulling over the mementoes of his unending battle. Out in the Liverpool night I felt woefully inadequate; because I was just a traveller, not a dispenser of justice.

It was the eve of my departure from Liverpool and my search for the poet and sign-painter had been unsuccessful. No one seemed to have any definite clue as to his whereabouts. None of the many addresses I was given proved useful. In some places, he had been there the day before I called, or the day before that. Nobody could say when they would next see him.

As I packed my bags that evening, I reflected that perhaps all I'd seen and heard was what lay behind the red, gold and green – inner city decay, the African seamen and their resentful children, nostalgic and embittered immigrants, indelible but unconfronted memories of a savage past, Rastas trapped in the "the ruins of Babylon". The red, gold and green were, I thought, tribal colours in a tribally divided city. The people of Toxteth felt themselves excluded from the rest of the city, where the other tribes roamed and each week celebrated and rejuvenated their allegiances at football matches. There, too, racial sentiments were stirred up, reaffirmed. The poet had demarcated Liverpool 8 because the rest of the city regarded it as separate. Yet the manner in which he made his statement was a profoundly Liverpudlian act. For in this city every tribe is represented in colours.

Then the telephone rang. It was the poet. "I understand you're looking for me," his voice said, against a noisy background. We arranged to meet in a popular wine bar in Liverpool's Bohemian area, which borders Toxteth. I was there within the hour. I'd seen a photograph of Leroy Cooper and recognised him instantly. He wore a black leather suit, and clutched a photograph album under his arm. A camera dangled from his shoulder. A leather cap partly covered thick strands of dreadlocks, which half-covered his face. It was an impish, mischievous face.

Over a drink, I asked the one question I had spent almost two weeks trudging through Liverpool to ask him. "Why did you paint the Toxteth street signs red, gold and green?"

He sipped his orange juice coolly and replied: "Well since the riots, people passing Liverpool 8 in their nice cars always stare as if they're passing a zoo. So I thought I'd give them a little clue about Toxteth. The red, gold and green."

"But most people haven't got a clue what those colours mean," I said.

"But you have," he said. "That's why you were looking for me. Anyway, it helps to liven up the place. It's so dull around here." And he smiled a smile of utter mischief, which caused me to laugh.

Leroy Cooper was born in Jamaica and brought to Liverpool when he was nine months old. At the age of twenty-five, he had served two prison sentences and considered himself a poet, photographer, dancer and musician. The photo album he held contained examples of his work. He allowed me to read two poems. One was a poetic appeal to Prince Charles, "the future king of England," to set his people free. The other was a tribute to David Moore, an invalid white youth who'd died under a police van in the 1981 riots. A line read: "We remember John F. Kennedy, Martin Luther King, Steve Biko. . . . But who remembers David Moore?"

Cooper's work embodied the spirit of Liverpool 8 – the harmony between black and white, the area's resentment of the rest of Liverpool, and the creativity crying out for recognition.

After our drink we strolled into Liverpool 8. Leroy pointed to a building which he claimed was the headquarters of the city's Masons and said: "One day, I'll paint it red, green and gold, too." Crossing over Parliament Street, into Princess Road, he showed me more evidence of his handiwork. A graffiti read: "Love life, love Liverpool". It had been his entry in a newspaper competition for a city slogan. The readers voted it top, but the judges settled for something with a more commercial appeal. Along Princess Road, we passed numerous churches, the base of the slave-owner's statue destroyed in the riots, a black and white couple strolling together, and two youngsters haggling over some unseen object. Liverpool 8 was preparing to sleep, to forget its troubles momentarily.

The poet and I parted half-way down Princess Road. And we knew we would meet again.

3. Interlude: Night in the Pennines

The Liverpool to Manchester motorway was clear of traffic. Only the regular pockets of dense fog restricted our speed. My companion and driver rocked his head to the throbbing music that issued from the radio. The lyric was simply "Jack, jack your body". It had a compelling beat, but the words were lamentable. I recalled the days when pop lyrics conveyed a message. But I knew the record being played would be a hit. And I felt regrettably old.

Manchester was a lot closer than I'd expected. One moment it seemed we were on an empty motorway, the next we were snarled up in traffic. The city sucked us towards its centre at a slow, tortuous pace. Then the traffic eased and we were in Piccadilly. We ate lunch in a modern café with uncomfortable seats. The waitress was a tall, elegant black girl. She was a sign that we were in a different kind of city. I hadn't seen a single black person working in central Liverpool.

We got lost leaving Manchester and ended up in neat suburban streets with houses that reminded me of Harare in Zimbabwe. My companion, Carl, said no matter how often he drove this route he always got lost. Back on the right road we passed Asian school-children hurrying home through the cold. Then past Glossop, the road began to climb. Walls made of a rough stone ran beside it, sometimes ending in houses built from the same material. Where the road widened snow which had been cleared formed thick, solid walls. Lorries hurtled past and made hissing, snake-like noises over the wet asphalt. We stopped at a camping site for Carl to relieve himself. I got out and looked around at the sloping land with its tiny fir trees and frozen heather. The air felt crisp and fresh in the winter afternoon.

We turned off the A57 – the snake pass Carl called it – and drove along a narrower, empty road. Snow walls now ran on both sides. Then the road began to rise with a sudden steepness. It climbed and twisted upwards as far as I could see. To our left was a precipice and beyond that a harsh, sparsely vegetated land rocketed upwards as if from the bowels of the earth. Then the road plunged, but continued winding like a discarded piece of string. I sighed at the rows of light in the distance. Civilisation again, I thought, thinking that we'd driven for almost five minutes without passing another car. In the valley below us were frozen lakes that seemed like great pools of mercury. At my request we stopped briefly again. A few sheep were picking over the icy grass and they returned my glances with rustic indifference. Behind them the land rose in a series of immense steps, like a giant staircase for some prehistoric behemoth. It was a beautifully austere land and it made me realise how little of this country, my adopted home, I'd seen.

Holmfirth was nearing the end of its working day as we entered it. I found an hotel. Carl had other arrangements. A girl in Holmfirth was expecting him that night.

After resting I had dinner. Later I went out into the night and discovered that a river ran beside the hotel. It produced a gentle music. I'd bought a book on Marcus Garvey from a Liverpool bookshop, and I spent the evening browsing through it. I woke up to the sound of the River Firth and went out into the chilly morning air. A thin mist hovered above the houses on a distant escarpment. I heard the sound of water rushing over rocks. And for a moment I felt that England was yielding a little of its secrets to me.

Carl had to be in Sheffield by half past nine. So we were on the road early. We drove up and out of Holmfirth and through undulating farm land broken up by narrow roads. A large, possibly man-made, lake appeared later on. Then the road began to plunge, the traffic thicken and the air lose some of its crispness. We were entering another city.

4. Sheffield: Blues on the Hills

Sheffield wasn't entirely unfamiliar to me. I'd been there in the early Seventies. It had left memories of giant chimney stacks billowing grey clouds into an even greyer sky, tiny, squat, terraced houses without front gardens, and people who spoke a quaint, almost archaic form of English. Mercifully there have been one or two changes.

Sheffield is just one of many northern cities that have been devastated by industrial decline. Up until the early Seventies it was the centre of British steel production. The city's craftsmen enjoyed an enviable prestige in the manufacturing of cutlery. Those who didn't work in the steel mills worked in the Yorkshire coal mines. Today, most of the steel mills have closed down. Foreign competition forced rationalisation, which in turn threw over 100,000 out of work. The mines, of course, weren't unaffected.

Paradoxically, Sheffield's industrial misfortune has also been its blessing, at least environmentally. The steel furnaces no longer cast their dark shadows over the city. The air isn't laden with soot, the raindrops are no longer acid. Recently, Sheffield had even won a European environment award.

Because Sheffield was never a grand city, the effects of the recession aren't immediately apparent. Unlike Liverpool, it has no great buildings to serve as festering sores of decay. In fact, there's an air of prosperity in its fashionable shops, its new pedestrian subways, and its discreet old buildings which blend well with the more modern architecture. Its Crucible Theatre is a vision of post-industrial leisure. In one afternoon there, I saw more working-class types than in a decade of going to London theatres. Whether they saw its plays, as opposed to making use merely of its cafeteria, was another matter.

To a traveller, the Sheffield people seemed friendlier and far less aggressive than their Liverpool counterparts. A court case in progress while I was there involved members of the Animal Liberation Front. The defendants were gentle, bearded young men who had the unhealthy pallor of health food addicts. A local reporter covering the case told me that Sheffield figured prominently in the national fight for animal liberation, a fact which may not be unconnected to its two city farms.

By night Sheffield has a unique charm. Its shopping and commercial centres are surrounded by hills, so one is always walking up or down, seldom on level ground. The street-lamps form intricate patterns that radiate outwards and upwards, like a bouquet of electric flowers.

The city has a small black community, comprising mainly Afro-Caribbeans, and a sizeable number of Somalis – surely one of Britain's most silent minorities. Originally, the black community was concentrated close to the city centre around Havelock Square, one of the Yorkshire Ripper's haunts. But the impressive municipal planning which enables Sheffield to hide its economic wounds dispersed that community. City planners acted quickly in response to the inner city riots of the early Eighties. Sheffield wasn't affected, and to pre-empt such occurrences the Havelock Square area was earmarked for redevelopment. Many black people were rehoused elsewhere.

But a community is more than the physical space it occupies. The language, shared memories and cultural habits of a people constantly demand expression. The authorities recognise that and have given Afro-Caribbeans a venue on the edge of the city. It's frequented by middle-aged Afro-Caribbeans who are contented to pass their evenings playing dominoes and cards. The younger generation, though, continue to visit the old haunts. An Asian mini-cab driver introduced me to Havelock Square. An illegal club called Mack's was where it all happened, he assured me. He didn't go there himself, because "when you have a family my size you haven't got time for things like that".

Mack's looked like a converted warehouse. Its clientèle were mainly black youngsters and their white girlfriends. Occasionally a few university students, distinguishable by their déclassé clothing, went there. Why it attracted anybody at all escaped me. Everybody seemed bored and restless as if they'd rather be elsewhere. The eponymous Mack was a quiet Jamaican in his early thirties. Mack had been trying to secure a club licence for four years. His failure didn't stop him operating the club, though. And the steady trickle of customers proved that there was a demand for his services. Perhaps one reason why Mack's licensing application had been unsuccessful was his minor criminal record. As a teenager he had been a devoted follower of Sheffield Wednesday, one of the local football teams. He learned early that to survive in a gang of football supporters required fighting skills. He became a distinguished hooligan, following his team throughout England. "The day wasn't complete without a punch-up, win or lose," he recalled.

But Mack's black skin made him conspicuous amongst his fellow white supporters. The police were always picking him out. "Might sound weird," he told me, "but I didn't think about me colour then. Only when I'd been nicked a third time that I realised why I was always the one who got caught."

Brief spells in remand centres introduced Mack to boxing. He took it seriously and won several competitions. But an eye injury soon ended his promising career. So far Mack's life seemed to have been an unending series of disasters, and it showed in his melancholy appearance.

Boxing remained one of Mack's passions. One afternoon we visited his former gym. It was on the other side of town. The journey took us through an industrial estate. For almost a mile we drove past workshops and factories festooned with "For Sale" signs that told their own sorry story. Then, as the road began to climb, we passed an immense stretch of wasteland, acres of rubble where a steel plant had once stood. Smouldering fires sent up wisps of smoke from amongst the broken bricks and wood and pieces of machinery. Funeral pyres, perhaps, to appease the angry gods of industry. Further on we stopped and looked down into the desert of industrial despair. Beyond it was Sheffield city centre. "When I was a kid," said Mack, "you couldn't see anything for miles from here. The smoke. This place was like a nightmare after Jamaica." Mack had spent his early years in the Jamaican countryside and he was one person who wasn't mourning the slow death of the old Sheffield.

The gym was in an old church hall, opposite a fifteenth-century church. It was run by Brendan, an Irishman with twinkling blue eyes and a wily smile. Himself a former boxer, his gym had put Sheffield on the boxing map. Two of his boxers – both black – were reigning European champions.

He'd lived in Sheffield for twenty-eight years, and had come straight from Ireland. In his early days, he told me, the

Irish were the blacks. "They were considered thick, Paddies who only had the sense to dig up roads. The locals despised us."

In the Seventies the surrounding neighbourhood had become a breeding ground for the National Front. They had blamed Sheffield's rising unemployment not on the recession but on the city's small immigrant population. Brendan was asked to stop black youngsters using his gym. He refused. "After seven hundred years of English rule, as an Irishman I couldn't subscribe to that."

He spoke with a gentle Irish accent and at a rapid-fire pace which made me think he must have kissed the legendary Blarney stone. Boxing had taken him all over the world. From his experience, it united the races and taught mutual respect. "Sometimes," he said, "a white boy comes in and says he hates blacks and wants to beat them up. So I puts him in the ring with a black kid and the black kid starts moving left, right, shuffling back, and the white kid can't hit him. After that they become good mates. Thing about boxing is that it's about survival. Black and white doesn't come into it."

We were standing beside the ring. Two boys, one Asian, the other white, were sparring with an older boxer. Around the gym a mixture of Asians, blacks and whites pumped iron, skipped and shadow-boxed. The air was becoming humid and the smell of sweat stronger. Brendan divided his attention between us and his boxers. To those in the ring, he shouted "Keep moving. Don't get hit. The less you get hit the longer you stay in the game." Then he'd break off to tell us anecdotes intended to illustrate the racial harmony that boxing created. Like the occasion when he was in South Africa: "I goes into this posh restaurant and every race's there. Black, white, yellow, brown, the lot. So I says to the waiter, ''Ere I thought you didn't believe in mixing the races, you know, apartheid and all that.' The waiter looks around and says to me, 'Everybody in here's the same colour, sir.' So I ask him what colour is that. 'The colour of money, sir. Would you like a table?'''

Brendan was keen to impress and entertain us with his knowledge of the world, boxing, and his empathy with his black boxers. When I asked why so many black kids took up boxing and with such apparent success, his humour began to wear a little thin. "They've got a natural rhythm," came his reply without hesitation, as if it was a question he'd answered a thousand times. On another occasion I'd have dismissed this answer as mere myth, racial stereotyping, but such a retort seemed irrelevant in this setting of sweaty muscular bodies, of dreams being pursued through punishing physical routines. All that mattered was that the Irish trainer with the gift of the gab believed in the myth. And it had brought him success. It wasn't the place for challenging clichés.

Besides, some of the boxers made his questionable answer seem highly plausible. A black boxer with a gladiatorial build was pitted against a slow-moving, awkward, white opponent. Entertainment for our benefit. The black boxer was required to avoid being hit and not to strike back. He ducked and dived and shuffled and side-stepped in a series of movements that resembled breakdancing.

The pride of Brendan's stable was Herol Graham. He came in while we were there and Brendan introduced us. In his black leather jacket and accompanied by two admiring white youths, he had the imperious air of a champion. I'd heard Herol Graham being interviewed on television and he'd struck me as an articulate boxer. A rarity. So I arranged to meet him for a chat at his jewellery store.

Driving back with Mack I sensed that he was depressed. It was understandable. Boxing had once promised him fame and fortune. Now all he had was an illegal nightclub in an economically depressed city. Far from the gym and wasteland, his mood picked up. "Some of those guys", he said, "look good, but they're not fighters. They're dancers. They wouldn't last any time in a proper fight." I wasn't sure whether to interpret this as the well-informed observation of a former pugilist or the envy of a failed boxer. "Now Mohammed Ali, that was a boxer," he said, and we drove the rest of the way with him comparing former boxing greats.

I met Herol Graham some days later. He owned a jewellery store in the Sheaf Market. His directions hadn't been too precise, but I had no trouble finding the shop. He was a local hero and everybody seemed to know Herol Graham's jewellery shop. Polite and soft-spoken, Herol was as articulate in the flesh as he was on the screen. His boxing career began when a white boy called him names and challenged him to do something about it. He did, and won the fight.

Success was not without its problems for Herol. He received begging letters every day, but never replied to them. "I had to work bleeding hard for what I got," he said, holding up a plastered arm. A training injury. "I'm not special. Anybody can do it, if you're prepared to get up five in the mornings and train for six hours every day. A lot of black youths aren't prepared to do that. They'll sit around smoking ganja and talking about going back to Africa. That's frigging rubbish."

Africa had left Herol with an unpleasant experience which he could now laugh at, but not when it happened. "I was in Nigeria, right, and this bloke ask me where I came from. So I told him my parents came from the West Indies and I was born in England. He says to me 'You're a white man then. We're the real black men, us from the continent.'"

Why a Nigerian racial purist should have so upset him escaped me. Unless, of course, it was important to him that he found acceptance amongst Africans. Our conversation was frequently interrupted by customers or fans or both. The first was a white father and son. The boy also had his arm in a plaster and wanted Herol's autograph on it. He obliged and the boy left brimming with pride and gratitude. The next customer was a middle-aged white lady who wanted a discount on a piece of jewellery because, she claimed, her son had been to school with the European Light Heavyweight champion. He offered her a standard ten per cent discount and when she'd left laughed wildly: he was schooled in Nottingham and had only moved to Sheffield when he started boxing.

While Herol attended to a customer, I recalled that the only occasion on which I'd heard the phrase "black Englishman" used was in television sports commentaries. The adulation that Herol received from his customers seemed to suggest that sporting success was the only way for black people to cease being immigrants. It was a sad thought, and I left Herol Graham basking in the glittering silver and gold of his success, dazzled by the generous admiration of these ancient Yorkshire people. A fine drizzle was falling and I walked through it wondering how Herol would fare once he had – as was inevitable – lost his crown.

I met the Sheffield Kid in Mack's club. It was a Saturday night and he was practising alone on a snooker table upstairs. He was glad for somebody to play with. He played the first game with indifference and seemed more interested in finding out about me. New faces were rare in Mack's.

I'd by now perfected a verbal calling-card to allay the kind of suspicion I'd encountered so often in Liverpool. It didn't satisfy the Kid. He wasn't suspicious, but genuinely curious. He'd never met a black person in my profession, someone who'd lived and worked in Africa, and a Jamaican, too. His father was Jamaican and his mother English.

He was a tall, broad-shouldered youth with an unruly mop of dreadlocks which hid his eyes. Despite his height, beard and confidence, he was only seventeen. He'd spent all his life in Sheffield and he hadn't worked since leaving school the year before.

The Sheffield Kid was an extraordinarily good pool player. He had a stylish cool, and literally danced and sang as he played. Curiously, his songs were mid-Seventies reggae numbers. He would have been far too young to be buying records at that time, but it was his playing that mesmerised me. Before shooting he'd flick his dreadlocks from his eyes with a toss of his head. And what shots he made! Until my encounter with the Kid I considered myself a proficient pool player. He taught me the difference between proficiency and excellence. After the first game – which I came close to winning – I was able to make only two shots in games that seemed to finish before they'd started. I could only sit and marvel at his boundless confidence, his unaffected panache. He didn't have a bad singing voice either.

A mutual attraction developed as we played. I was perceived as a worldly wise stranger in town, and this endeared me to him. He was a local boy who had ambitions to escape Sheffield for an imagined exciting world outside. I soon found myself playing big brother, offering advice.

Three games after telling me of his plans to leave Sheffield, the Kid revealed why he was still there. His girlfriend had recently had a baby. He was proud to be a father. That was obvious. But fatherhood wasn't without its problems. The child's mother was his age and still lived at home. Her Jamaican parents were devout Christians. They staunchly refused to allow him in unless he shaved off his shoulder-length dreadlocks. They'd even tempted him with the offer of a trip to Jamaica. He wasn't budging, though.

"It's her mother," said the Sheffield Kid with suppressed anger. "She's the one who stopped me from going to the house. Father's not bothered really."

We decided that it'd be a good idea if he started wooing his child's grandmother. He had to show her that his Rasta hairstyle was no reason for not accepting him, especially now that he was an in-law of sorts. Besides, he wasn't a real Rasta. His dreadlocks were grown when he hung out with a Rasta group. "After a while I realised they were talking rubbish," said the Kid. "All that talk about going back to Africa. They won't do ought." But he was fond of his dreadlocks and would cut them off in his own time, never under duress.

"Maybe I'll take her some flowers one day," the Kid mused aloud, "red, gold and green ones."

I laughed and agreed, but told him he'd have difficulties finding green flowers.

The arrival of other pool players limited our conversation. One was a middle-aged black man with a plump white lady wearing dangerously high stiletto heels. Gold chains hung from his neck, and his fingers glittered with more gold. They played silently on the only other table. It seemed that playing pool in Mack's was their Saturday night out.

Although the club played some excellent music – classical reggae and soul numbers – it didn't pick up as the night wore on. The Kid was beaten by another player about his age. He took it well and we went downstairs to the bar.

Bored-looking black youths and young English girls with

badly made-up faces stood around the dance area. These girls, the Kid told me, would hang around Sheffield for a few years, learning the game. Some might drift into permanent relationships with a pimp. The more adventurous ones would head for London – Park Lane or Soho.

"There's no money in Sheffield," he said flatly. "Maybe once they've made enough money, or been arrested a few times too often they'll come back to good old Sheffield."

The Kid, who only drank Lucozade, introduced me to a friend of his. Older than the Kid, he was also of mixed race and looked vaguely Mediterranean. He was called Paul, and hearing that I lived in London he asked if I knew Brixton. I told him I'd lived there for two years.

"Do they put something in the water over in Brixton, then?" he said, half-serious, half-joking. He went on to recount his one and only experience of Brixton. Two black youths had followed him for half-an-hour and then tried to mug him in a record shop. "Were after my gold," he said, holding up a left hand weighed down by four thick gold rings. He escaped and swore never to go there again.

I said Brixton took a while to get used to, and maybe he shouldn't flaunt his wealth in certain places.

The Kid suggested we went to a shebeen. I didn't know what a shebeen was, but after his explanation realised that it was a blues dance: a house party where drinks and food are sold. The blues the Kid had in mind was on the other side of town. So we left Mack's to find a taxi.

As we walked, I asked him if there wasn't a black nightspot in the city centre. There wasn't. And, according to the Kid, many black youths avoided the city centre on week-end nights. He claimed that the police discouraged them from going there to prevent fights with their white counterparts.

"And it's the white guys who always want to start fights after a couple of beers," he sucked his cheeks in disgust, like a true Jamaican annoyed at something or someone. "It's like the police are saying that white boys and girls can use the city centre. But not us. Know what I mean? Stupid really. When you tell somebody not to do something like that, they're much more likely to want to do it. So a lot of black guys still go there on Friday and Saturday nights. Good luck to them. That's all I say."

His attempt at contemptuous indifference didn't hide the hurt in his voice. He was a Sheffield boy by birth and upbringing, yet he was also an outsider. I'd detected a greater racial tolerance in Sheffield, but, if the Kid was to be believed, it shared some of Liverpool's cruelties.

"Same with football," said the Kid, as if reading my mind. "Go to a game and they wanna beat you up because you're not white. I mean, you're there to support the same team. Stupid innit?"

He began singing a reggae song, and walking in step with the beat which played in his head. Hands in his pockets, he moved with a mixture of dance and swaggering motions. He was young and there was still much to understand in life, meanwhile – he seemed to be saying by singing – his songs enabled him to survive it all. All around us, the street lamps rose upwards, disappeared down valleys, then reappeared still climbing, as if to the sky.

Most blues I'd been to took place in dimly lit, claustrophobic basements. Not the blues we went to that night. It was on Rock Street, and we got in by climbing some dangerously steep steps. They led to a house perched on a ridge. A blues on a hill in Rock Street!

It was 2 am, and the Rock Street blues was in full swing. A visiting sound system had attracted a full house. Guys in sharp suits and gold chains leant against the corridor walls. And well-dressed young women, both black and white, squeezed to and fro. It took us twenty minutes to secure a space in that sweaty, smoky and dark interior. The Kid seemed to know everybody, and when he'd finished his hellos got down to some serious dancing, dancing the way he played pool – cool and stylishly.

I stayed in the dance rooms as long as my lungs could take it. Then I went to stand in the corridor. A female voice behind me asked for a light. I turned round to face a large Asian girl with long black hair. I was surprised.

She accepted my offer of a drink. In the time I spent with her, I learnt that she was born in Bradford. At fourteen she ran away from home and drifted around various northern cities. Sheffield was now her home and Afro-Caribbean culture a way of life for her. I didn't get much further. Her boyfriend, a smooth-looking Rasta with a baby face and dressed in a three-piece pinstripe suit, came and took her away.

As we left the blues, the Kid invited me to meet his family. I took up his offer the following day. He lived with his parents in Parkhill, a monstrous council estate towering behind Sheffield's sole railway station. Walking along its corridors I couldn't imagine a more alienating environment. Suicides, baby batterings and mental depressions are, I learnt, common problems. The Kid told me that sometimes he was woken up at night by animal-like screams. They'd last for hours then stop as abruptly as they'd started. Days later he might learn that a couple had been fighting. Mostly, though, the sources of the nocturnal screams remained a mystery.

"Just one of those things," he said nonchalantly.

His home was minimally furnished. All the furniture was old. Not one item was there for decorative purposes. A Bob Marley poster, along with various reggae album sleeves, adorned the walls. It was warm. Parkhill is heated by an ingenious conversion scheme which transforms rubbish into heat. It's a cheap system which allows the council to provide heating for eighteen hours daily.

Although I was in Yorkshire, hundreds of feet in the sky, I felt as if I was in a Jamaican tenement yard. And his father added to that feeling.

Ken MacDonald, lanky, lean and bearded, spoke and moved with a tropical languor. Meeting him explained the Kid's love affair with Jamaica. Ken had come to Sheffield at the age of sixteen. Though he'd long left Jamaica, Jamaica clearly hadn't left him. It was only in recent years, he said, that he'd stopped dreaming about the island of his birth. He doubted that he'd ever be able to return there.

Ken was a troubled man. None of his three children had so far shown any sign of living up to his ambitions for them. The Kid had never worked, and his brother, a year older, was drifting around in a gang. He feared that it was only a matter of time before the police came knocking on his door. He saw college as their only hope, but he couldn't motivate either of them. His most urgent concern was for his daughter. She was only fifteen and had already stopped attending school. She said the teachers were hostile towards her, and showed no interest in her progress. He'd been to the school several times. Nobody there could explain his daughter's attitude. He was baffled, because at a younger age she'd been a voracious reader. What alarmed him most was her advice to him. She'd told him pointedly not to worry about her, because the state would look after her. She'd shaken him, left him fretful, disorientated. He hadn't taught her to think that way.

Ken's dilemma highlighted an aspect of Sheffield which, as a visitor, I wouldn't have noticed. It's a Labour stronghold.

Has been for decades. No other British city has built as many council houses. Its citizens may not be wealthy. But they don't go wanting. Food, housing and clothing are guaranteed. But this caring socialism happens alongside a devastating industrial decline. Sheffield's local government, perhaps one of Britain's most enlightened, has cushioned people from the loss of their jobs, but it has not been able to create enough new jobs. Sheffield's socialism is a crutch for the victims of capitalist industrial collapse. It is not an alternative to the capitalism of which the city leaders are so critical. This is the limitation of localised socialism in an overwhelmingly capitalistic national context.

One immediate and disturbing consequence is that a whole generation is growing up without ever having experienced work. They have got into the habit of thinking that, come what may, the state will provide. I am most certainly not a Conservative supporter. But my discussion with Ken made me realise that perhaps there was some usefulness to Norman Tebbit's unpopular advice to the unemployed: "Get on your bike." The problem is, though, that Sheffield is surrounded by cities experiencing a similar economic malaise. There are no greener pastures in the North.

The Kid's sister came in while I was there. She was accompanied by a tall, straight-backed elderly woman, who turned out to be their grandmother. She was grumpy. She never smiled once, and spoke with such a strong Jamaican accent that I wouldn't have guessed that she'd lived in England for over twenty-five years. Mrs MacDonald had good cause to be grumpy. She was on her way to church and had stopped in for a particular reason: her granddaughter. She wanted to know why the child had stopped attending school. And what was Ken doing about it?

She wagged her finger at him, insisting that he was responsible for the child going astray. "From you was a bwoy," she said, "me send you go a school, and when you didn't wan' go me beat you to go. Now you have children, you telling me that you can't make them go to school. Bwoy, is what kind of son me raise?"

As she spoke Ken, a forty-odd-year-old father of three, became a boy again. He could say nothing to appease her, to convince her that he was as concerned, if not more than she was, about his children. With Ken effectively bludgeoned into silence by her words, she asked for the children's mother. The Kid's sister told her that their mother was out visiting a friend. "Visiting!" Mrs MacDonald exlaimed. "How she can go to other people's yard when she have so much problems in her own? She should be here. You better tell her I want to talk to her. Me no know how she can tell pickney not to worry 'bout work."

It seemed that the Kid's mother was more lackadaisical about her children's future. Her father had died from a common coal-miner's illness, and she'd often told them that "Work kills".

"You ever hear anything like that, Mister," she said, turning on me. I quickly replied that I hadn't, but thought that the Kid's mother wasn't entirely wrong. Though it was strange advice to give children.

The Kid had gone upstairs to wash his hair. He entered the room as his grandmother was at the height of her angry sermon. He strolled over to her, still drying his dreadlocks with a huge pink towel. This formidable Jamaican pensioner turned to him and barked: "And you, Mister, I don't want you coming up to me in the street with that hair of yours. I tell you before, is only madmen carry them themselves like that in Jamaica."

The Kid handled her invective rather better than his father. He smiled a wickedly endearing smile and put his arms around her. And I could see his irate grandmother struggling to resist his charmful guile. She then turned her anger instead on the Kid's defenceless sister.

Ken, his chin in his hands, his eyes to the floor, as if wishing it would open to allow his escape, gave a long-suffering sigh. Before leaving, Grandmother again reprimanded him for not being more disciplined with his children. Her departure left a fleeting stillness, like the aftermath of a storm. The Kid looked at his father with a curiously aged sympathy.

Ken MacDonald was under pressure from all sides. There just seemed no way out. He himself was unemployed, and it seemed soon the entire family would be queuing up at the unemployment office. On top of that he was being blamed for a failure which was only partly his fault – his children's lack of education. But he wasn't alone. So many other families, especially Afro-Caribbeans, are in the same boat.

A little while after the old woman had left, he became less despondent. He apologised for his mother's intemperate performance. I said it was all right because I'd seen shades of my own father in her.

Night was falling and we went to stand on the balcony. It gave a panoramic view over central Sheffield. The undulating street lights, some still flickering on, were a momentarily beautiful distraction. Behind us, the Kid had put on a reggae record. A hoarse, lugubrious voice moaned in lamentation:

> "And they carried us away from Africa
> With the intention to steal our culture. . . ."

I knew the song, but not its title and tried to recall it. But
the Kid's father sighed with weariness, breaking the silence
between us, and said: "True words, and we don't know
when our tribulations will end." And I forgot about recalling the title of the song.

I persuaded the Kid to take me to visit his grandmother.
We met outside the town hall on a Friday afternoon. A flock
of starlings had colonised a tower on the old town hall
building. Their chattering created a discordant music above
the traffic noise. Pensioners and office workers waited
patiently at the bus stops. Soon the city centre would be the
playground of the young, those with money to spend. The
Kid wasn't one of them, he was planning on spending the
evening in Mack's.

On the way I asked him about his other grandmother. He
was surprisingly reticent. She'd moved to Blackpool and
seldom visited Sheffield.

Mrs MacDonald lived alone in a two-up, two-down terraced house. We entered by the back door. She wasn't
exactly pleased to see the Kid, but she wasn't hostile
either. Within minutes she was criticising his hair and
general appearance. The Kid listened on sufferance, then,
when the opportunity arose, explained why he'd brought
me there.

She frowned and said: "Me no know 'bout no interview,
but you is a friend of me grandson. So you is welcome."

We sat in a dimly lit dining-room. Fading black and
white family photographs hung on the wall. They were of
her many daughters' weddings and, from the style of
clothes, must have been taken in Jamaica. Other photo-

graphs on the mantelpiece showed her grandchildren, those in Sheffield and those in Jamaica and the United States, where three of her daughters lived. The mandatory plastic flowers and plaster casts of ducks in flight were also evident.

Mrs MacDonald's presence in Sheffield was but the latest stopping point for a family with a long record of migration. Her own mother had worked in Panama for five years. She sold provisions to the workers, many of whom were Jamaicans, on the Panama Canal. Ill-health brought her back to Jamaica in 1912, but she never stopped talking about Panama and the money to be made there. As a child Mrs MacDonald often heard stories of uncles who'd fought in the First World War. Some never returned.

"Even at the age of seventy-five," she said, she "couldn't understand why ordinary people who had nothing to do with the start of de war should go and fight. Mek them who start war go and fight."

One of her sisters lived in Cuba for twenty years. She returned to Jamaica and built a headstone for her mother's grave, which the family hadn't been able to afford. Then she built a house in Kingston. "Don't look like me going to see her again," Mrs MacDonald said wistfully, "Every morning me wake up Jamaica seem a likkle further away."

She said if ever I was in Jamaica I should look up her family. The MacDonalds were famous in Westmoreland Parish. She had more family than she knew about. Apparently, according to family legend, all the MacDonalds were descended from a Scotsman who owned a slave plantation during slavery. Free to fornicate with his female slaves, he left innumerable offspring.

"Now me think of it," she said thoughtfully, "all this time me inna Sheffield, me so close to Scotland and me never go there." And she gave a cackling laugh. Then she served us Jamaican cocoa tea and sweet potato pie, and the Kid asked for more.

5. Birmingham: Blades of Frustration

The train journey to Birmingham was uneventful. A long night of playing pool at Mack's had left me exhausted, sleepy and a little irritable. The heat in the carriage and the uniform flatness of the Midlands landscape contributed to my drowsiness. Only a more rugged terrain – like the Pennines – would have kept me fully awake. Consequently, much of the journey passed in a nether-world: unexciting blurred images; the seemingly whispered conversations of my fellow passengers. It was the sight of old, disused engine workshops in Derby which brought me back to the real world. As the countryside resumed, I realised I was feeling apprehensive about my next stop. Birmingham and I were no strangers. I had lived and worked there for almost a year. It had been a profoundly disturbing experience.

In 1980, after six uncertain months out of university, I finally secured a job. A national charity concerned with penal matters employed me as an educational researcher. I was attached to a project in Handsworth, Birmingham. My brief was to write a report on the educational background of its clients – young black offenders. My duties seemed simple enough. It was not exactly the career I had in mind, but like many graduates from working-class backgrounds, I had no definite career planned. And I was young, enthusiastic and filled with that youthful optimism which owes much to a lack of worldly experience. In short, I was prepared to try my hand at almost anything.

As part of my induction I spent a morning in Birmingham's Victoria Law Courts. The first case involved a white petty criminal. To the magistrate he showed deference, remorse and had to be restrained from making endless apologies. He had been caught committing a crime and was resigned to being punished. He affected a humility that was intended to win a light sentence. Part of the legal game. The black defendants, however, refused to play the game. Without exception, they were young, Rastas, and fiercely defiant. It was clear, to me at least, that they did not recognise the court's authority.

The first Rasta defendant was charged with burglary. He dismissed the magistrate as an "agent of Babylon" unfit to pass judgement on him, a child of Zion. Soon, he warned, Babylon would be destroyed by thunder and lightning, brimstone and fire, and "the downpressors of Jah's children" would perish. The court ushers hauled him away, and the stony-faced magistrate wearily called for the next case. This, too, involved another Rasta. His mother was in the gallery. She was middle-aged and clearly distraught, holding a handkerchief to her face. The boy looked on disdainfully as the lawyer attempted to convince the magistrate that his client came from a decent Christian home. He was granted bail and a probation report ordered in time for his next appearance. All the subsequent defendants that morning were black.

Back in the office, a little terraced house on the edge of Handsworth, I daily interviewed youngsters who had been to borstal, detention centre, or prison. Incarceration is supposed to rehabilitate as well as punish. None of my interviewees showed any signs of repentance. They had simply endured their punishment as part of the expected "wickedness of Babylon". A recurrent complaint was that certain institutions forced them to shave off their dreadlocks. Rastafarianism was not a recognised religion. Punished, but neither repentant nor rehabilitated, they drifted back into the lifestyle that had led them to jail. Their separation from the black community had begun when they became Rastas. Now they were ex-criminals as well, living in communal squats which subsisted on dole-cheques and stolen food. Babylon, they believed, owed them a living. Spiritual sustenance was provided by collective Bible-reading sessions.

They had all left school, some prematurely, without any qualifications. This meant they were ill-equipped to compete in a shrinking job market. Not that they were interested in work. They made a conscious effort not to "toil for Babylon system" and described their hardworking parents as "brainwashed servants of Babylon".

Imprisonment was, perhaps, the mildest form of punishment. Worse was internment in a mental home. Handsworth is served by All Saints', a manorial building looking out on to landscaped gardens. It had a fearsome reputation. Those who ended up there, it was widely believed, were condemned to a lifetime of insanity. If you went in sane, you came out crazy; and if you went in crazy, you came out crazier.

None of the custodial institutions I visited compared with All Saints'. Mental home internees are known as patients, not prisoners. It is a misleading euphemism. Many black people end up in mental homes through the courts. Insanity is as much a legal as it is a medical condition.

I once visited a boy who had been sent to All Saints' some weeks after I met him. He was barely recognisable. The drugs used to keep him docile had blown him up like a rubber ball. His eyes were vacant, his mouth frothy, and he had difficulty staying awake.

Prison or mental hospital: that was the choice which seemed to face the first generation of Afro-Britons. Explanations and accusations were plentiful. The police, the magistrates, the prison warders and the doctors were condemned as racists by radical critics. But they deflected criticism by blaming the schools which had turned these youngsters loose. The schools in turn blamed Afro-Caribbean parents for not exercising enough discipline at home. And the parents? They were simply baffled.

But there was one area of agreement between the police, the courts and black parents: Rastafarian ideas and practices were opposed to law-abiding behaviour. It encouraged a type of non-conformity which led to criminal actions.

I was less ready to blame Rastafarianism. To do so seemed more like an exercise in prejudice than an explanation of the problem. But I could offer no alternatives. Maybe I was too close to the project's clients. Less than five years separated me from them; and we came from similar cultural backgrounds. I had also experienced the anger that marked black adolescence, that inspired rebellion against white authority, that made Rastafarianism appear attractive. What was it about being black and young in a white society which encouraged rebellion? An answer eluded me.

Initially, I felt like a nurse in a battle zone. It was my duty to repair the lives of young men engaged in a mysterious war against society. I tried doing my best, though I believed that the only way to end the flow of decimated lives was for the war to end. That was beyond my power. And, each passing day, I became more disillusioned, more convinced that I was temperamentally unsuited for this kind of work. My working environment exacerbated this feeling. All my colleagues were, like me, black and university graduates. Our secretary suffered from eczema and her sensitive skin condition was a barometer of office tension. She became increasingly bed-ridden.

The project leader's conduct kept staff morale low. He was a woefully inadequate leader. He commanded little respect and his efforts to exercise authority heightened his unpopularity. One day I had to intervene to prevent him being beaten up by another colleague.

The frustration of the job, compounded by internecine office conflict, created an intolerable strain, whittling away my enthusiasm. I began to yearn for the day when my contract would end. I did not want to be in Handsworth, witnessing the tragedy of a generation, lives destroyed before they had been lived. But Handsworth's problems were not unique to it. They were happening in most black communities. Within a year of my departure, the inner city riots erupted all over Britain.

White, unevenly spaced tower-blocks appeared on the horizon like giant up-ended domino pieces. Minutes later the train came to a smooth halt in the gloomy, whitewashed interior of New Street Station. I remained seated until the carriage was empty, mentally preparing myself for a visit which was long overdue. The knot of apprehension in my stomach had begun to loosen with my recollections. The station concourse was so brightly lit that it hurt my eyes. My bag handle was causing me a minor discomfiture. I dropped the bag on the marble floor. By standing still the swishing crowd, of which I'd been part, suddenly seemed to slow down. To my right, I noticed a heated argument between a middle-aged Asian and smartly dressed young black man.

"Give me my money, now," the Asian insisted. "Four pounds, please."

"I told you I was just gonna get some change, didn't I," the black man said. His long white coat and tilted, broad hat gave him a vaguely American appearance. It contrasted with his black British working-class accent.

"Why were you going for the platform?" the Asian said. "I saw you. Give me my money now."

The black man grinned and looked around furtively, as if contemplating flight. "All right, all right, come with me, then. Bloody hell, it's only a few quid. Why would I want to skank you a few quid." He led the way towards the booking counter, the Asian stuck close to him. I suspected that the Asian was a mini-cab driver, the black man his passenger.

I picked up my bag and walked to the escalator. Above New Street station is a shopping complex. Entering it now, I recalled the many altercations I had witnessed here between unemployed youngsters, black and white, and security guards. Its bright lights, warmth and window displays of clothes, furniture, tropical holiday scenery – all the things the unemployed cannot afford – made it a popular place for loitering. The guards tried to keep them moving. As I made my way to the exit, I noticed several groups of youngsters who were clearly loitering. The security guards, though, ignored them. It seemed that the Bull Ring was no longer an area for conflict between the have-nots and the guards of the haves.

Birmingham has both improved and deteriorated since 1980, when it shattered my youthful optimism. Then, factories were closing down every day, and unemployment figures could be likened to the temperature of a fever-ridden patient; frighteningly high, and still rising. It gave this city of workshops – many of which dated from the industrial revolution – an atmosphere of desperation. But Birmingham appears to have survived the worst. A new civic pride prevails. The many construction sites in central Birmingham threaten to enhance further the city's futuristic appearance. Looping underpasses and flyovers form a concrete maze that can confuse a stranger. Even taxi-drivers here seem a little uncertain of directions. With its international airport, giant exhibition centre, its mushrooming conference venues, its symphony orchestra, Birmingham takes its "second city" status seriously.

Reminders of Victorian Britain are all over Birmingham. It acquired its city charter a year before Queen Victoria's birth. A modest, but centrally located statue of the Queen who, for many Britons, personifies all that was good and great about Britain, watches over the city from Victoria Square. The older public buildings around it are grand, imposing. Their architectural styles reflect the national confidence that marked Queen Victoria's reign; the decades when the red, white and blue of the Union Jack fluttered over more than half the globe.

On my second day in Birmingham I broke my glasses and took them to be repaired. The optician, a smooth, voluble man of indeterminate age, suggested I visit the canals. There, he said, I would see the factories and workshops built in the decades when "Birmingham was the workshop of the world". He often took his family on canal walks, and they would try to imagine the lives of the people who used to work there, making the trinkets and buckles and guns that earned Birmingham its industrial fame. "Sixteen-hour working-day then," he said. "We're lucky to be living now and not then." He was one of the first ordinary Englishmen I had met in years whose romance with the past was counterbalanced by an awareness of its more unpleasant aspects.

I said I would get to the canals, but, regretfully, never did. The cafés and dives and inhabitants of a part of Birmingham of which my optician acquaintance confessed total ignorance – except through media reports – were far too absorbing. That part of Birmingham was Handsworth; and its character also owes much to the age of Empire.

Handsworth begins about a mile from central Birmingham. Former colonial subjects and their British-born children are everywhere in Birmingham. But Handsworth is the city's main immigrant quarter. In fact, it is the largest single concentration of Asians and Afro-Caribbeans in Britain. Handsworth's fame, or infamy, rests mainly on its volatile Afro-Caribbean population. But they are outnumbered by Asians. A main shopping area is Soho Road. This is a mile-long stretch of shops where Asian-owned take-aways, restaurants, greengrocers and cheap novelty shops create the strongest impression. Windows full of sweets and Indian clothes create a riot of colours. Beside them the native-owned shops are unremarkable, easily forgotten.

When some schools close in Handsworth, the pupils who stream out of their gates are overwhelmingly Asian. Elsewhere in the neighbourhood, old churches and other large buildings now house Hindu and Sikh temples and Muslim mosques. Here, as in most places where they have settled, Asians are an exclusive group. Deeply divided by caste and religion among themselves, they are nonetheless impenetrable to outsiders. Their exclusivity is a strength. But it is also a weakness because it arouses hostility in people whose culture is more accessible, like the Afro-Caribbeans.

Thousands of miles from the colonies, decades after colonial rule, the ex-colonials act out on the streets of Handsworth an old conflict. Mutual suspicion and mild contempt mark the relationship between Afro-Caribbeans and Asians.

I experienced the gulf between these two occupants of the same inner city space many times. One afternoon, as I strolled through a Handsworth back street, noting its suburban-type houses – pockets of Handsworth can appear quite out of place – an Asian woman gave me a disturbing look. She had sensed my presence late. She pulled her two young children close to her, and I saw fear in her eyes, as if she was expecting me to attack.

Afro-Caribbeans resent the Asians' exclusivity. At times I heard remarks which echoed sentiments I heard on a visit to Nairobi, Kenya, in 1985. "The Asian shopkeeper over-charges." "He only employs his family or fellow Asians." And, of course, "Don't look at their women. They'll come for you with daggers."

The Asians' highly developed and self-contained culture has contributed to their startlingly impressive commercial success. But some of their British-born children probably find it too rigid. Its rejection is not unusual. I had seen Asian punks in Birmingham city centre, and in Handsworth I saw an Asian Rastafarian. And a young Asian taxi-driver shocked me when I asked him to turn down the music in his car. It was reggae, and it was far too loud. He replied: "Wha' 'appen? The I don't like the music? No problem, man." An act for my benefit, or a genuine instance of cultural migration?

In years to come Handsworth could resemble Caribbean islands like Trinidad and Tobago. In those places Asians have mixed with their African neighbours, contributing to the creation of a unique island identity. But for now the two races are divided by suspicion and fear. A latent conflict simmers below the surface. Handsworth still bears the ugly scars of September '85 when that conflict exploded, when the muted resentment of blacks was given violent expression.

Over two nights black youths clashed with the police. In their rampage, the rioters singled out Asian shops. Several were burnt down. On Lozells Road, rows of shops end abruptly at wastelands where Asian-owned shops once stood. Otherwise Handsworth life is back to normal.

Lozells Road is the heart of black Handsworth. It teems with people throughout the day. Social care agencies appear at regular intervals along with Afro-Caribbean take-away food shops and mini-cab offices. By day BMW cars, the ultimate symbol of inner city success, cruise up and down. Many bear red, gold and green pennants beside the national colours of particular islands. Jamaica's yellow, green and black is most common. Occasionally, you see the Rasta colours next to the Union Jack, signifying, perhaps, a dual allegiance, an emergent sense of being both black and British, with all the contradiction and tensions that go with such an identity.

The Nightspot Café is the busiest on Lozells Road. I remembered it as a tidy little place where I sometimes ate lunch. It has changed almost beyond recognition. Food is still sold there, and lots more. Everybody seems to carry knives, which they brandish about like toys, creating a tense, violent atmosphere. The knives are used. Many people, young men at that, bore scars, on foreheads, on cheeks, on chins and, in one instance, across a neck. Death, I suspected, was a common visitor. And madness, too. One young man stood against a wall staring into space with bulging, flame-red eyes. Nobody saw him. He was an invisible man. Around him quick furtive deals were struck under the benign gaze of Jamaica's national heroes on a poster – Marcus Garvey, Paul Bogle, George William Gordon, Bustamante and Norman Manley. The two pool tables were never unoccupied. They were stages for performers crying out to be seen and

admired. The pool table made or broke reputations, confer-
ring a limited fame on steady winners, and shame on luckless
losers. Sometimes its electric light illuminated the blade of
frustration and the blood of discord.

At night the pace slows down on Lozells Road. The cafés
close and those who make their living in the shadows retire
home or hang out in the blues dances. There, it is said, you
can tell the cocaine sniffers because they are the only ones
still dancing at seven and eight in the morning.

I haunted these dives and cafés for a few days in the hope of
coming across some familiar faces. That was how I met two
former clients on Lozells Road. One had shaved off his
dreadlocks. With his grimy face and blue overalls, he was a
picture of the working-man. He was hurrying back to work
on a building-site, so we didn't get much chance to talk. The
other was still committed to Rasta, at least in appearance. He
didn't remember me. I had to prod his memory.

"Oh yeah, what was that project called again?"

I reminded him and asked what he was doing with himself.

He'd been friendly so far, but now his tone changed. He
said bluntly: "Well I don't rightly know that I should tell
you that, cause I hear that you guys used to work for the
police. All that talk 'bout helping black youths was a
cover-up."

I was shocked, wounded with indignation. I, who'd
perceived myself as a helpless nurse, was now viewed by the
people whom I'd tried to help as an agent of their enemy.

"Who told you that?" I demanded.

"Well as I is not a informer, I can't tell you that. Is what I
hear. But is not everything I hear I believe, know what I
mean?"

I was relieved but far too upset to continue the conversation. We'd met walking in opposite directions. And that was

the way we went. I simply told him: "It's a good thing you don't believe everything you hear."

I couldn't remember his name or exactly what dealings I'd had with him. But for the next few days his accusation troubled me. It forced me to begin thinking about 1980 not from the perspective of a personal ordeal, but from that of my so-called clients. The youngsters I worked with in 1980 belonged to the first generation of British-born blacks. That so many seemed to get in trouble with the law reflected a crisis which was partly located in British society, and partly a legacy of Afro-Caribbean culture.

Britain in the 1970s was a nation struggling to come to terms with its loss of Empire and diminished world stature. Without the controlled markets of the Empire, its industries were proving unprofitable. They were unable to compete in a freer international market. National self-confidence was at a low ebb. A crisis of moral, social, economic and political dimensions had set in.

This national climate generated different responses from different groups. Nationalism and racism, kindred spirits reared their ugly heads amongst whites. Fascist political movements committed to keeping Britain white proliferated. Whites became more paranoid about immigrants than they had been in the previous decade.

This upsurge in British nationalism and racism had very real repercussions on Afro-Caribbeans. Their responses took many forms. Some West Indians who had been here for decades returned home. A black travel agent in Handsworth told me that between '79 and '83 Caribbean shipping and travel agents enjoyed a minor trade boom.

"Business hasn't been as good since," he lamented. "One week in '82 we had over fifty people making enquiries about returning home. That's a lot. Maybe half of them came back and completed the procedures. Now I can't remember the last time I had a customer returning home for good."

The returnees were mainly workers who had been made redundant. Their redundancy payments and early retirement provided the means for the return journey. Their motives for leaving Britain were complex. Many had only seen Britain as a temporary home. Five years was the standard time immigrants gave themselves to mine Britain's street of gold. The hostile national climate of the Seventies probably served to remind many that they had over-stayed.

Equally disturbing to older West Indians was the conduct of their British-born children. Rejected by a Britishness which excluded blacks, the first generation of Afro-Britons retreated into a blackness which rejected Britain. That blackness was Rastafarianism. Back in Jamaica, Rastas were the outcasts, the dregs, the insane of society. To see their children embrace this apparently bizarre cult drove many older West Indians to distraction. The movement that captured the imagination of a generation is no longer so popular on the streets. But its outward trappings – hairstyle, language and colours – are still common features in Handsworth.

After some searching I managed to find a group of Rastas, as opposed to those who merely assume Rasta style. They were part of an international organisation known as Twelve Tribes. I met them in a youth centre in Winson Green, which neighbours Handsworth. Their spokesman was called Captain. He had the most beautiful eyes: brown, clear and sparkling. His parents were Jamaican and he was obviously a mixture of African and Indian. Captain was reluctant to talk about Twelve Tribes, insisting he had no authority to speak on behalf of the organisation. But he was prepared to speak in a personal capacity.

He had been converted to Rasta in 1979, when he was sixteen. A Twelve Tribes meeting in a local park convinced him that the movement should be taken seriously. Since then he had lived for Rasta. The brethrens met twice a week, and once a month they organised a function, which included music and "reasoning sessions".

While we spoke other members filed into the room. The men formed small groups. The women occupied a distant corner.

"Twelve Tribes", Captain said, "doesn't deal in racial divisions. Anybody can join." As if in response to this statement, a white girl entered. She wore a long, colourful skirt, and her head was covered. She joined the other females, who, from what I could make out, were exchanging recipes.

Captain reaffirmed the basic tenets of Rastafarianism: the Bible is the book of life, Africa is the motherland and all Rastas should be repatriated there. He himself was looking forward to the day when South Africa was freed, and, ideally, would like to live in Ethiopia.

"There's nothing, nothing here for us," he said, his bright eyes smiling. "The West is heading for disaster. Reagan and Thatcher are just two signs. It's all in the Bible. So is repatriation we dealing with. Africa. Cause we don't want to be here when Armageddon come."

Much of what the Rasta leader had to say I had heard over the years. It was all stale, clichés from another decade. For a moment it seemed to me that everybody in that room was trapped in time. The Eighties, with its emphasis on materialism and making it, had left them untouched.

The hours I spent in the Rastas' company reminded me of just how powerful the movement was once. Afro-Britons now entering their adolescence are less likely to embrace

Rastafarianism. But they will enter a world in which the movement has had a lasting impact.

Captain's repeated reference to Africa provides the key to understanding why West Indian parents were so uncomfortable with Rastafarianism. The British national climate of the '70s generated the need for a defence of blackness. That it took the form of Rastafarianism was a consequence of certain peculiarities in Afro-Caribbean culture.

The "West Indian" immigrant regarded Britain as the mother country with a passion unrivalled by any other postwar immigrants. Asian immigrants were merely exercising their legal right as British colonial subjects to reside in Britain. On the whole they retained a sense of loyalty to a culture which owed little to British influence. The "West Indies", on the other hand, believed they were exercising a birthright. Not just a legal right. And in a crucial respect they were correct. For the West Indian was a British creation. They were the bastard offspring of a violent encounter between a young, vigorous nation of avaricious maritime merchants, Britain, and an ancient continent, Africa.

A people, like a nation, are their memories, Afro-Caribbeans no less. An Afro-Caribbean is a descendant of those African slaves transported to Caribbean islands between the middle of the sixteenth and the early part of the nineteenth century. West Africans from diverse ethnic backgrounds were involved – Yorubas, Ibos, Mandingoes, Ashantes and so on.

From the moment of capture the African ceased to be a human being with a language, a history, a culture. He became a piece of property, branded with, for instance, Liverpool's famous DD mark. The physical horrors of the Middle Passage and the relentless cruelty of the slavery regime are well documented. Even I, generations from it, find it painful to learn about.

Slavery was also a psychological ordeal. That aspect has been given less thought. But we know that the African – the Yoruba, the Ashante, or whatever – ceased to be what he was. The slave regime forced him to speak his master's tongue. He answered to a name given him by his master. Later he came to worship his master's god. And because all men make God in their own image, he worshipped his master. With each new generation the slave's collective self-esteem appeared to erode. New slaves arriving from Africa were derided by those they met on the island. An African was a person to be mocked. In mocking the new arrival, of course, they were also mocking themselves.

In *The Middle Passage*, the Trinidadian writer V. S. Naipaul quotes Anthony Trollope's observation on post-slavery West Indians:

> They have no religion of their own, and can hardly as yet be said to have, as a people, a religion of adoption. The West Indian knows nothing of Africa except that it is a term of reproach.

Naipaul himself observes: "This was the greatest damage done to the negro by slavery. It taught him self-contempt."

My own father, at times, exhibited a similar trait. In moments of anger he would admonish me as a "Kwaku". For years I regarded Kwaku solely as a term of disapproval. Until I met a Ghanaian called Kwaku. Amongst the Ewes in Ghana, I learnt, it's a day name given to boys born on a Wednesday.

Somewhere in Jamaica's distant past, Kwaku was a newly arrived African slave. Those born into slavery probably considered his behaviour foolish, troublesome, awkward.

And so the name Kwaku became a term of reproach: its original meaning lost in the slave culture that was forging a new personality. Yet my father couldn't be described as a man lacking in self-pride. He is dark, powerfully built and self-consciously handsome. Self-hatred or blind emulation of whites were never a part of my upbringing. Does that make Naipaul's observations supported by several nineteenth-century European travellers wrong? Not entirely.

The harrowing process, lasting almost three centuries, that transformed the African slave into a West Indian colonial was bound to have deep and long-lasting effects. The most serious was that it left the African, now "West Indian", with a profound ambivalence towards his Africanness. His was a divided personality, the product of a violent and divided culture. Events in the 1970s forced an examination of that past, that culture. Racial memories were stirred up.

One afternoon I went to meet the owner of a pirate radio station. Music Master, as he is known, runs the People's Community Radio Line. A Jamaican in his early forties, he told me of his long-running efforts to get black music played on local commercial and public stations. Frustrated by the station manager's intransigence, he decided to start his own. In the station's five-year history it has been raided over a hundred times, losing thousands of pounds' worth of equipment to the police. But the station enjoyed such widespread support, that he always managed to return to the air within a few hours. On one occasion, a Birmingham vicar even allowed the station to broadcast from the belfry.

Music Master, the radio pirate, was an example of persistence and commercial cunning. His DJs were young blacks who could never get work on mainstream radio, and his advertising customers were local businesses who could not afford the mainstream rates.

As I left the building, I was struck by a poster near the entrance. I had seen the picture in a book, but never on anybody's walls. It was an eighteenth-century slave auction advert, depicting an African slave with a grotesque, four-pronged shackle around his neck. After listing the slave's qualities, the poster enumerated various commodities for sale, like sugar and rum.

My host had disappeared to resume his work. I asked his young assistant, who stood beside the poster, why anybody would want to use an image of that terrible phase in history as decoration. She replied, "That's what we were, innit?"

Slavery did not completely destroy the African's attachment to Africa. During slavery the idea of Africa became synonymous with freedom, dignity, resistance. It inspired many slave rebellions. This explains another side to the West Indian personality: an irrepressibly powerful urge for Africa, a spiritual yearning for the land from which he had been forcibly exiled.

The Cuban writer, Alejo Carpentier, in his *Kingdom of This World*, based on the San Domingo revolt, provides a moving description of the slave's attachment to Africa. A slave revolt leader has gone into hiding. The slaves await his return:

> One day he would give the sign for the great uprising, and the Lords of Back There, headed by Damballah, the Master of the Roads, and Ogoun, Master of the Swords, would bring the thunder and lightning and unleash the cyclone that would round out the work of men's hands. In that great hour . . . the blood of the whites would run into the brooks . . .

A violent imagery for a violent situation. This urge for Africa was given innumerable expressions in folklore. For example, it was believed in the Caribbean that when a person died his spirit would return to Africa.

Caribbean spiritual songs, evoking biblical imagery, similarly reflected this longing. One such song, set to a disco beat, was an enormous hit in the pop charts in the 1970s:

> By the rivers of Babylon, there we sat down
> And there we wept when we remembered Zion.
> For the wicked carried us away into captivity
> Required of us a song,
> But how can we sing King Alpha's song
> In a strange land.

The same pop group, comprising Afro-Caribbeans, had an equally successful chart hit with another folk song – "Brown Girl in the Ring". This expressed the other side of the "West Indian" personality. Its refrain went:

> Brown girl in the ring tra-la-la-la
> There's a brown girl in the ring tra-la-la-la
> And she looks like a sugar in a plum.

The brown girl was the "mulatto". Closer to European standards of beauty, she was admired by her black – and by West Indian definition – less fortunate playmates. The lighter you are in complexion in the Caribbean, the more privileged you are likely to be. That was so yesterday, and it remains so today.

The "West Indian's" dual personality is most evident in literary writing. The work of Claude McKay, a Jamaican novelist and poet, who came from a peasant background, is an excellent example. McKay was one of the first poets to use Jamaican dialect, precursing the dub-poets of the Seventies by almost seventy years. But where dub-poetry has radical artistic and political connotations today, in McKay's usage it expresses a colonial's yearning for "Old England":

> I've a longin' in me dept's of heart dat I can conquer not,
> 'Tis a wish dat I've been having from since I could form a t'o't,
> Just to view de homeland England,
> in de streets of London walk,
> An' to watch de factory chimneys pourin' smoke up to de sky,
> An' to see de matches-children, dat I hear 'about passin' by.

McKay's imaginative sojourn reaches its climax in a visit to "de lone spot where in peaceful solitude, rests de body of our Missis Queen, Victoria de Good."

Eight years later, though, having moved to America, McKay has adopted a more orthodox style and now makes a soul-felt plea for his race and Africa:

> Oh, when I think of my long-suffering race,
> For weary centuries, despised, oppressed,
> Enslaved and lynched, denied a human place
> In the great line of the Christian west;
> And in the Black Land disinherited,
> Robbed in the ancient country of its birth,
> My heart grows sick with hate, becomes as lead,
> For this my race that has no home on earth. . . .

This complex, contradictory West Indian personality, torn as he was between the mother country of his master, and the motherland of his ancestors, came to Britain in the post-war years. His panama hat, sunshine smile and cardboard suitcase concealed a wounded psyche, a divided self.

"West Indian" writers accorded monumental significance to the migration. The Barbadian writer, George Lamming, speaks of Caliban coming to meet Prospero. "Yet Prospero is afraid of Caliban. He is afraid because he knows that his encounter with Caliban is, largely, his encounter with himself."

Lamming perhaps exaggerates. But he points us in the right direction. The West Indian and British personalities were inextricably entwined. Their encounter on British soil, in a more enlightened age, would expose each other's weaknesses. Illusions and fantasies would be tested.

Britain in the Fifties was unfit to receive the West Indian immigrant other than as a unit of labour. He had no history beside British history, no culture beside British culture. And the West Indian, desperate for work, fleeing rural poverty for the bright metropolitan lights wanted to believe that he was British. The racial attacks of Nottingham and Notting Hill in 1958, the racial prejudice that confined him to the poorest parts of the city and gave him the lowest paid, and least secure work – these were the rewards of patriotism. But the West Indian immigrant could withstand it all. He could look forward to the day when he could return to the West Indies.

His children were another matter. The West Indies, for those born there and brought here at a young age, were nothing more than vague, fragmented memories. For those born here, it was a place learned from stories told over paraffin-heaters in one or other British city. The British-born or -reared black, inheritor of a slave legacy that involved both self-contempt and a longing for Africa, began to graduate from British schools from the late Sixties. However strong his inherited love for the mother country (i.e. Britain), it could not be sustained. Only the most determinedly self-destructive person could continue to believe unquestioningly that he was British. For the most part, mother and child embraced and recoiled in horror.

For Britain also had a legacy, a legacy of slavery and empire that determined how it viewed all non-whites. That legacy pervaded every aspect of British life. It was ingrained in the British personality. Schools taught British imperial history which denigrated Africans, Asians and Chinese. Books which had educated and entertained Britons contained insulting stereotypes of non-whites. Television and newspapers daily portrayed grossly derogatory images of foreigners. And the darker their skin, the worse the image.

Wherever the black British youngster turned he was confronted by hideous reflections of him or herself. It was as painful as walking barefoot on broken glass. It was a lonely, alienating childhood, a baptism of fire.

Adolescence is a difficult period for any child. It can be an age of many searching questions and too few answers about the world that you have inherited and your place in it. The questions asked, the answers found, are part of the passage to adulthood.

The black adolescent's questions invariably focus on identity. Either he can accept society's ugly reflection of himself and become resigned to taking up the role it has allocated him – that of a menial worker – or he can challenge both reflection and future role.

The school-leavers of the late Sixties and early Seventies were immeasurably assisted in mounting that challenge by Afro-American civil rights and black power movements. The literature, music, films and so on were imported into Britain. Sometimes they came via the Caribbean. For instance, a popular reggae adaptation of an Afro-American tune, "Message from a Blackman", had the lines: "I am black, that's no reason to hold me back. You're white, that doesn't make you right."

But rebellions are seldom exportable. And Black Power and the Civil Rights movement, however relevant to black Britain, were American phenomena. They were the political expressions of a people who, rightfully and confidently, believed in their entitlement to a share in the American dream. America, a nation of immigrants, was as much theirs as other ethnic groups'. The Afro-Caribbean migrant's belief in his Britishness was far less secure. Nevertheless, the Black Power influence was beneficial. It encouraged educational pursuits. And for those who doubted that there would ever be an opportunity to make use of their education in Britain, there was always the option of returning to the Caribbean.

Black Power was, however, short-lived in Britain. It was quickly overtaken by an intimately related, but quite distinct, phenomenon – Rastafarianism. As the Seventies progressed, an increasing number of black youngsters, now-British-born, fell under its influence. It promised answers to all their questions of identity. And it did so from within a West Indian slave tradition. It was the most powerful modern expression of the urge for Africa.

Black Power made political demands and encouraged political organisation. Black Power followers also looked to Africa for inspiration. The Afro-hairstyle, the dashiki pilgrimages to Africa were a few ways the Black Power adherents acknowledged their African heritage. But Africa wasn't just acknowledged in Rasta ideology. It was the utopia to which they sought physical repatriation. Babylon, the west, was beyond redemption. It was inexorably headed towards Armageddon. On that judgement day, the Rastas would be free to return to Africa. Meanwhile, Rastas simply opted out. One of the Rastas I talked to when I was working in Birmingham told me how he would get to Africa on that great day: "By foot, bus, some will fly. Jah will guide. 'Cause I-man know that Africa will be free by 1983."

This fatalism was what most disturbed me about Handsworth in 1980. I could understand the forces that made Rasta attractive. I'd experienced them myself. But, having grown up in the shadow of the Sixties and Black Power, I believed in the possibility of change, of a better tomorrow. Here, in Handsworth, it was as though a whole generation had lost all hope in that difficult transition from boy to man, girl to woman.

But Rasta was never without its virtues. It forced the British-born black person to confront a part of his heritage which his parents had largely shunned. It shattered the West Indian's British identity, releasing an urge for Africa that had been long repressed. For those who did not succumb to the fatalism inherent in Rasta's mystical vision of racial redemption, it was a cathartic experience: a spirit freed.

The Rasta revolution was nothing more than a generation's awakening. Here in Handsworth it has stirred a flowering of artistic talents. Birmingham is richer for it. Freed to explore the African aspect of their culture, the first generation of Afro-Britons have tapped a creative source of immense potential. Poets, painters, sculptors and musicians abound in Handsworth. At least two African drum and dance companies originated in Birmingham in the late Seventies and early Eighties. Though repertoires are based on rhythms and movements acquired on journeys to the Caribbean and Ghana. In central Birmingham one Saturday afternoon I noticed a group of Rasta artists selling their wares outside the Bull Ring. A popular poster depicted Bob Marley, John Lennon and Marvin Gaye.

But on the other side of this coin of collective self-discovery are criminality and mental disturbance. The Handsworth frontline is also a thriving ganja market, a twenty-four-hour affair. Conducted openly in cafés and on the streets, it invites regular police raids. There is something suicidal about overt defiance. As one Jamaican mini-cab driver told me: "Mahn, I know those guys have to make a living, but to do it so openly. They just asking for trouble."

Mental disturbance is less obvious but just as serious. The self-discovery that Rasta prompts can also be a route to mental disorder. Not every individual can survive a rude awakening. In embracing the Rasta ideals some are driven by a mania for evangelical conversion. They become prophets. And Handsworth, I was told, overflows with modern race redeemers.

It is possible that during my stay the appalling weather kept these self-styled prophets off the streets. I saw only one. Dressed in ill-fitting trousers, no socks, a woollen hat that looked like a stove pipe, he stood on a street corner muttering something about the wrath of God.

But my informant, a social worker, didn't exaggerate. Almost thirty per cent of the inmates in Birmingham's All Saints' hospital are black. The national average for black inmates of mental hospitals is roughly seventeen per cent. Both figures are very alarming when you consider that Britain's Afro-Caribbeans are less than three per cent of the population.

The culturally and legally determined criteria of mental disturbance undoubtedly play a part in producing these figures; inner city poverty also. But perhaps more attention should be given to the peculiarly extreme dilemma that is intrinsic to Afro-Caribbean culture. Africa and Europe seem to have been at war within it for four hundred years. Every person of Afro-Caribbean origin carries that conflict within him or her. In the moments when there is a retreat into blackness – whether or not it takes the form of Rasta – the African's past and present conditions in the west can assume a deadly importance. Black self-realisation so easily becomes ensnared in yesterday's humiliations, yesterday's shame. The resultant anger is sometimes immensely creative. But it can also swiftly progress to an uncontainable rage against all whites. And by definition it is also directed inwards. For like the person of more immediate mixed-blood white hatred is tantamount to hating a part of one-self. We all walk a tightrope of normality, but for a black person the risks of slipping – or being pushed – are greater, the fall more precipitous. Maybe that is why one of the most common words in black street talk is "Pressure". It has social and economic connotations, but it also refers to the powerful psychological struggle involved in holding the two, often warring sides, of the one personality together.

One afternoon I wandered around Birmingham Art Gallery. My aesthetic criterion is uncompromisingly simple: I must be able to face the object of art first thing in the morning.

Jacob Epstein's "Rock Drill" would mean waking up to a science fiction nightmare. It will haunt me for a long time. A looming humanoid shape, with insect head, of a metallic, manufactured quality, stands with its legs wide apart, gripping a drill or a monstrous weapon. It is entirely white, a sleek, harsh whiteness. What was Epstein trying to say? Was this his vision of the future, man and his machine of production and destruction almost indistinguishably fused, one resembling the other? Man the grim machine without compassion, without a heart, an extension of the object he made, a purely functional creation programmed either to produce or destroy or both: man without a soul. Or is Epstein warning us, before it's too late, of the dangers of a progress impelled solely by the profit motive and the market which demands that technology be perpetually re-invented, overlooking a fundamental fact: that the machine should serve people; not vice-versa. Obsessed by mechanical and electronic inventions is man inventing himself out of existence? Or is Epstein's machine creature merely a resigned acknowledgement of the fact that in using tools to recreate our world, as we've always done, we are constantly recreating ourselves? Which ever, it's not a vision of future man I'd like to see.

Jock McFaddyen's huge, untidy, satirical paintings of inner-city life touched me in a different way. They were instantly recognisable: Asians, Europeans and Africans occupying the same claustrophobic space, going about their life chores. But McFaddyen's inner-city dwellers are exaggerated to the point of sheer ugliness: short; hideously distorted features. I would dread having to wake up to either artist's vision of the world. It is neither just "nasty, short and brutish" as McFaddyen seems to imply; nor the gloomy vision of Epstein. But these versions of reality are no less real because I dislike them, or, more accurately, because I couldn't live with them.

Outside the art gallery, I ran into a familiar figure. He stood in the shadow of Queen Victoria's statue, waiting for someone: oddly out of place with his bright, intense eyes, and ingrained look of suspicion. His name was Beany, and

I'd met him briefly in 1980. He ran a black self-help group in Handsworth, and was well known for his radical black nationalist politics. A small, brown-skinned man, he had a permanent aura of hostility and aggression. Back in 1980, he was a figure who struck fear in the army of white academic researchers who used Handsworth as a race relations laboratory. I recalled that he wasn't too fond of black college graduates either.

I hesitantly went up to him. To my surprise he was quite friendly. He told me of a meeting on Marcus Garvey that his organisation was holding next day. I accepted the invitation beside the pigeon-soiled statue.

The meeting was being held on Heathfield Road, which runs at right angles to Lozells Road, and meets it at Villiers Cross, the centre of the 1985 unrest. A little way into Heathfield Road, I found myself walking behind a woman dressed in West African clothes: a bright red, gold and green scarf wrapped round her neck. I was intrigued. The damp, cold February weather was hardly suitable for tropical clothing. I caught up with her and, pretending to be searching for the venue, asked for directions. She told me what I already knew, that I was on the right road. It wasn't far.

"Aren't you cold dressed like that?" I asked, as we strolled side by side.

"I'm an African," she said. "So I dress like a African." Her accent combined the rhythms of the Caribbean and the Midlands.

"Yes, but in weather like this you need some solid English clothes," I said.

She laughed and said: "When you know your African identity, the cold can't bother you. Only when you is a African and you don't know it that the cold bite you."

Beneath her laughter was the gravity of belief. She was defying the cold, asserting an identity she'd discovered in Handsworth. I laughed with her, but a little uneasily.

We parted when she went down a side street. Further on I came upon "The Culture Shop". Its window display was a chaotic selection of books, magazines, pennants, African carvings and dashikis. I went in to browse around. The meeting, I knew, wouldn't start on time. The window display had been an accurate reflection of the shop's contents. It was all familiar. A similar shop in Ladbroke Grove had provided me with an alternative education in my early teens. A Rastaman was behind the counter. The only customer was a young white man. He was trying on a woollen red, gold and green hat. He scrutinised his reflection in a small wall-mirror, pulling the peak over his eyes, then pushing it backwards. He was clearly uncertain whether it suited him. Finally, he turned to the Rasta shopkeeper and said: "What d'ya think. Is it me?" He could have been in Marks & Spencer.

The Rasta, with a calm serenity, stepped back, assumed a thoughtful pose with one hand under his chin, and answered: "Yeah, mahn. Is you all right. All de way."

The customer was pleased. He bought the hat, and left the shop looking like a boy who'd just purchased his first bicycle.

I asked the Rasta if the shop attracted many white customers.

"Quite a few," he said. "Mostly for the t-shirts, though. You know, with Bob Marley and ganja leaf. But more and more a them buying the hats."

"So business is good," I said.

"Well, me bredda," he said. "Truthfully speaking business can never be good inna Babylon."

The Marcus Garvey meeting was held in the basement of a semi-detached house. Upstairs were pictures of Marcus Garvey, Malcolm X, and African Liberation posters from Mozambique, Angola and South Africa. A small room contained a photographic exhibition of pictures taken by the organisation's members in Ethiopia. They'd gone there, bearing aid collected from the Handsworth people.

It was a small planning meeting to organise events to mark the centenary of Marcus Garvey's birth – he was born in 1887. Delegates representing black organisations throughout Britain were present. They were school teachers, community workers, artists and social workers. It seemed that an earlier meeting had discussed the significance of Garvey, and the need to celebrate his centenary. This meeting was purely technical.

The chairman, green-eyed and red-skinned, with a pronounced Jamaican accent, was firm. Ideological discussions were quickly squashed. He had little choice. The basement, a dance venue at week-ends, wasn't the ideal place for a discussion which if allowed to run, would have been interminable. Consequently, the meeting left me with little understanding of what Marcus Garvey meant to the participants. But it was clear that 1987 would be the year when Garvey's ideas would be separated from the mysticism of Rasta. After the meeting broke up, I spoke to one or two of the delegates. Some I'd known in the past and lost contact with. As I spoke to a painter whose work I'd once admired, an elderly gentleman joined us. His impish, wrinkled and golden face was redolent with delight.

"Mahn, I can tell you," he said, placing his hands on our shoulders, "how pleased I am to see you youngsters here. Is a sign of how far we come that you all know about the greatest black man that has lived in the twentieth century."

"Did you know Marcus Garvey?" I said.

"Not exactly," he said. "I was only a boy in Jamaica then. But some of my family knew him. You want to hear a story 'bout Marcus?"

My acquaintance and I nodded.

"Well, when Marcus married his first wife, Amy Ashwood, I hear my auntie say to my mother: 'But what a way the man black and ugly. How a pretty gal like 'er could marry 'im, me don't know.'" He chuckled lightly and added, "That's the Jamaica I was born in. You all don't know how lucky you're not to have been born there." Having told his story, he ambled off, still chuckling to himself. A strange old man, I thought.

Marcus Mosiah Garvey personified all the contradictions and paradoxes of the West Indian personality. He gave it a vast, dramatic expression. His stage was the whole world. The reverberations of Garvey's work are still being felt today. In many respects, the black British children of the inner cities are Garvey's children.

Marcus Garvey was born less than fifty years after the abolition of slavery, and three years after the Berlin Conference where the European powers carved up Africa between themselves. Jamaica was then a colony ruled from London through a Governor General. The recently freed blacks subsisted at the bottom of the social hierarchy. Between the blacks and the white rulers were the "mulattos", the children of slave masters and slave women. The mulattos despised the blacks, who in turn were ambivalent about their identity.

Garvey came from a reasonably well-off Jamaican peasant family. His father, a stone-mason, kept a library. His mother was a devout Wesleyan. Garvey read avidly from his father's library, and later from books kept by his uncle, to whom he was apprenticed as a printer. Early in his teens he had his first experience of the issue that would dominate his adult life – race. A white playmate of his, a Wesleyan preacher's daughter, was sent away from Jamaica and ordered never to contact him again. Garvey wrote later: "It was then that I found . . . that there was some difference in humanity and that there were differences in races, each having its own separate and distinct social life."

Garvey's early racial awareness made him restless. At eighteen he moved to Kingston. There he threw himself into a frenetic range of activities, rapidly developing a reputation amongst Kingstonians as a social worker, political activist and publisher. He took elocution lessons, and learned four new words every day. At twenty-one, he launched the first of many publications – the *Watchman*. But Jamaica was too small for young Garvey. So in 1910 he left on a journey that took him through central and South America. Thousands of Jamaicans and other English-speaking West Indians were then working on the Panama Canal. They lived and worked in almost inhuman conditions. Garvey started two more publications along the way, aimed at black workers who, throughout the region, were being exploited.

In 1912 Garvey landed penniless and alone in London. After working his way around Britain – Cardiff, Liverpool, Edinburgh – he returned to London, and took a job on *The African and Orient Review*. In Jamaica he'd been exposed to regional Black Nationalist ideas, but working for this journal introduced him to the writings of Black Nationalists from the United States and Africa, and also gave him an appreciation of anti-colonial struggles in Asia. He became a great admirer of Mahatma Gandhi.

. . . I make no apology for prophesying that there will soon be a turning point in the history of the West Indies; [Garvey wrote in the journal] and that the people who inhabit that portion of the Western Hemisphere will be the instruments of uniting a scattered race who, before the close of many centuries, will found an Empire on which the sun shall shine as ceaselessly as it shines on the Empire of the North today.

With the threat of war in 1914, Garvey returned to Jamaica, and it was during the passage home that he was inspired to form the Universal Negro Improvement Association (UNIA). With the motto, "One God, One Aim, One Destiny", it was launched in Jamaica on August 1st – Emancipation Day in the West Indies. The early UNIA had the limited objective of moral and social improvement of black Jamaicans. On his travels Garvey had everywhere witnessed the denigration of his race through colonialism and, he believed, their own shortcomings. The UNIA sought to uplift the race, while fostering unity and brotherhood between the races. He was encouraged by the colonial establishment, but condemned by the Jamaican middle classes. They regarded themselves as coloureds and not Negroes, a term of disparagement in their circles. They left Garvey with a bitter dislike of "tainted" Africans.

Frustrated at home and desperately in need of funds for his fledgling organisation, Garvey left for the United States on a fund-raising tour in 1916. This move was the turning-point in his career. The United States of America had from 1910 been in the grip of racial unrest. Blacks fleeing southern poverty and Jim Crow laws were flocking to the northern states. There they encountered mob violence from settled Americans and newly arrived European immigrants. When the war ended, black soldiers who'd fought for freedom and democracy returned home to unchanged social and political conditions. Black America was in turmoil. And so too were the British colonies.

Garvey's début in America was less than successful. He's said to have fallen off the stage on his first speech in Harlem, where he established a branch of the UNIA. But his message found a ready audience in disillusioned war veterans, and migrants from the south. By 1918 his now-successful UNIA was running a range of businesses, including hotels, restaurants, launderettes and a trucking business. It had its own newspaper, *The Negro World* which Garvey edited. The paper was distributed not only in the USA, but internationally. Black sailors, UNIA members and sympathisers ensured that *The Negro World* became the most widely-read black newspaper in the world. In a short time the UNIA had branches throughout the Americas and Africa. There were even UNIA branches in Ireland and Australia. South Africa had the largest number of UNIA branches in Africa. Many of the founders of the African National Congress were also Garveyites. From his first vague objectives, Garvey's thinking had now broadened. The UNIA's rallying cry became: "Africa for the Africans, those at home and those abroad." The organisation was to be the means of uniting the 400 million "Negroes" of the world into one nation, giving them a government of their own – an understandable goal at the time, since there were only two independent African countries: Liberia and Ethiopia. Everywhere else Africans were under European domination. But what would Garvey's brave new world of Africans look like?

At the 1920 International Convention of the Negro Peoples of the World, 25,000 thronged Madison Square Gardens to witness a spectacle unseen in Afro-America since. Amid much pomp Marcus Garvey was elected Provisional President of Africa, and President General of the UNIA, and leading delegates were bestowed with grand titles, such as: Duke of the Nile, Earl of the Congo and Baron of the Zambezi. Garvey's back-to-Africa project proposed a recolonisation of Africa by African descendants in the West. He had no vision of an alternative form of civilisation to colonialism, merely one that copied the West. He expressed it this way: "Until you can produce what the white man has produced you will not be his equal."

The black man, for Garvey, had to acquire the white man's will to dominate, and with it the white man's mastery of science and technology. And who better to do it, he seemed to imply, than one who had supped at the master's table, the former slave. History, in Garvey's world view, was a conflict between races; the black man – who'd once known glory – was destined to become the next world ruler.

But Garvey recognised nothing of value in black culture. It was all to be borrowed. "Spiritual and Jazz music," Garvey wrote, "are credited to the Negro, but it was simply because we did not know better." At no stage did Garvey question how Europe achieved world domination. Its only fault was that it oppressed Africans, denying them a government of their own. It was a serious flaw in Garvey's vision.

Yet Garvey achieved much that is praiseworthy. His UNIA secured an agreement with the Liberian government, that returnees from the West would be settled there. But the Liberian government, under pressure from the United States and the colonial powers, reneged on the deal and the land eventually went to Firestone, the US rubber company.

The UNIA also had its own shipping company, The Black Star Line, intended to rival Cunard's White Star Line. Four ships were purchased from funds acquired through public stocks bought by black People.

But even as he was triumphantly rising, Marcus Garvey was tragically falling. Singlemindedness, stubborn determination, and a confidence bordering on arrogance which had enabled him to build up his organisation were also his failings: he disagreed with everyone, white and black, radical and conservative.

His critics were legion. Afro-American race leaders, like W. E. Du Bois, envied Garvey's phenomenal success in mobilising millions. But Du Bois also charged Garvey with importing the "West Indian" race problem, with its obsession with pigmentation, into the United States. Graduations in colour, said Du Bois, were unimportant there: anybody with a trace of African blood was discriminated against. Moreover, Garvey's back-to-Africa call was tantamount to saying: "Give up! Surrender! The struggle is useless; back to Africa and fight the white world."

The FBI infiltrated spies into senior UNIA positions. And to pressure from within America was added pressure from the colonial authorities. *The Negro World* was banned throughout the British and French colonies. In some places, its possession carried a death sentence, and the British denied Garvey a visa to visit Nigeria.

His fall began in 1922 when he was indicted for using the US mail to defraud. His lengthy trial culminated in a five-year sentence in Atlanta prison. On his release after two and a half years, he was deported to Jamaica, where he was given an excited, enthusiastic welcome. But he was never to regain his former glory. London became Garvey's last home. He spoke regularly at Speakers' Corner, continued his journalism and publishing. He went for strolls in Kensington Gardens and recalled those halycon days of hope and glory. By now, he was a broken embittered man. In the spring of 1940 Garvey suffered the second of two strokes. The back-to-Africa prophet died without ever setting foot in Africa. In 1964 his body was disinterred and returned to Jamaica, where he became the island's first National Hero.

Beyond all the confusion and contradictions, Garvey's message to black people was "Up you mighty race, you can accomplish what you will." It was a battle cry that inspired millions. He gave people of African descent in the West a new vision of themselves and helped to destroy some of the mental effects of slavery. Today, there are few black community centres in Britain which do not have a portrait of Garvey on its walls. He has become an icon of black consciousness. But unless the emergent black Britons can transcend Marcus Garvey's "race first" philosophy, they will remain trapped in the castle of their skin.

One of the secrets of Marcus Garvey's extraordinary appeal was his spiritualism. His modern-day followers in Britain, however, appear to be uncomfortable with this feature of Garvey's life. He has become a secular figure. Yet the church was crucial to Garvey's success in mobilising millions. Garvey wrote: "If the white man has the idea of a white God, let him worship his God as he desires. . . . We Negroes believe in the God of Ethiopia [Africa], the everlasting God – God the Father, God the Son and God the Holy Ghost, the One God of all ages. That is the God in whom we believe, but we shall worship him through the spectacles of Ethiopia." In the USA Garvey's UNIA was closely aligned to the church, and had its own in the African Orthodox Church. When he was jailed, black churches throughout the United States held Release Garvey Sundays. If a public figure of Garvey's stature were to emerge today in Britain, the Church would play an equally central role. And it's in Handsworth that you see this most clearly.

The frontline of drug-dealers, battle-scarred youths, Rastas and social care agencies is only one face of Handsworth. There is another, and far more pervasive side, the Church. The two co-exist uncomfortably and seldom meet. Church events occur throughout the week. But it's at weekends that the churches come into life. From Saturday night, when the Seventh Day Adventists meet, the discerning listener can hear the mellifluous voices wafting from ancient churches long ago abandoned by their white worshippers.

Afro-Caribbeans brought with them to Britain a powerful tradition of spiritual worship. Birmingham alone has over a hundred black churches. And they're still growing. The most common are the New Testament Church of God and the Church of God of Prophecy. Their congregations are almost always exclusively black, though white faces are not uncommon.

More than any other black organisation in Afro-Britain, the churches operate at a national level. Conventions, usually with guest preachers from the United States, bring them together at least once a year. Between these conventions there are monthly and weekly visits to congregations in other cities.

The strength of the churches becomes apparent on a Sunday morning. Then Birmingham's black-run pirate radio station plays only gospel music from early on. Out on the streets hundreds of middle-aged men, women and children make their way to various churches by foot, bus, family car, or, most commonly, church-owned mini-bus. The women wear hats that are reserved for this occasion, hats that range from the almost flamboyant to the conservatively discreet. And the men dress in well-pressed suits that probably only see daylight on this special day. The large number of young people suggests that the church is far more powerful than is generally acknowledged.

I attended a black church service one Birmingham Sunday morning. It was on Lozells Road, opposite a café where on week-days ganja sellers ply their wares, and the Ackee Tree, a blues dance venue. The wicked, though, were nowhere in sight. They were resting from their own demanding worship to the gods of the night.

As I entered, a short, dumpy black woman, her eyes hidden by a red, saucer-shaped hat, handed me a Bible and a hymn-book. After signing the visitors' book, I took a seat. The church's interior was simple, almost spartan, and there were at least three hundred people in attendance. Behind the pulpit, which towered over the congregation, the choir chamber ascended to the back of the church. The choristers were all dressed in loose, brown gowns.

At the foot of the altar, five couples were having their babies baptised. With each baptism, the preacher exhorted the parents to rear the child in the Christian way. The baptismal part of the service concluded with a hymn from the youth choir.

After a reading of weekly notices, Pastor Thompson took over: a stocky, dark, balding man with narrow bloodshot eyes and a curiously cruel smile. His sermon lasted for over an hour. It was an amazing performance, accompanied by wildly gesticulating hands and constant pacing across the pulpit. He paused only to wipe his forehead, which glistened with sweat. Both preacher and congregation seemed to urge each other on. Throughout the sermon members of the congregation shouted "Hallelujah", "Bless the Lord", "Amen" and "Yes Lord".

I was sitting a few rows behind an elderly man. He seemed

to have a special rapport with the preacher. He stood up and remained there, intoning in a deep, gravelly voice charged with emotion: "Yes Lord. Oh, My Lord." A brown woman in a nylon cream dress also stood up and added to the plaintive echo. Her palms outstretched to the preacher, she repeatedly cried: "Yes Lawd. Yes Lawd."

The sermon moved effortlessly, despite the preacher's profuse sweating, from urging the young to be disciplined, ambitious Christians, to condemning the promiscuity of modern life. It upheld the sanctity of the family, stressing that, because women came from man's rib, they should be obedient to and supportive of their men. Men were urged to show respect and love for women.

The preacher then asked us to stand. He called on those who hadn't been saved by Jesus to come forward. The response was slow, but people began drifting towards the altar. They were young and old, male and female. They knelt at the altar's foot, below a bouquet of flowers, preacher and choir towering above them.

Preacher Thompson led the prayer, but people prayed individually and out loud, creating a cacophony of voices. And then the singing began. It started softly, like the musical whisper of wind blowing through trees; and it gradually grew louder until the entire church was filled with a heart-stirring rendition of "Follow Jesus". It brought more people to the front. One young man, his hair curly-permed and dressed in stylish Saturday night clothes, began sobbing.

I, who had never been much of a church-goer, had never heard such hauntingly beautiful singing before. I was moved. I was there as an observer, but those intensely soulful voices drew me into the worship. I felt my eyes moisten and my head go a little giddy, like the effect of the first cigarette in the morning on an empty stomach. It even entered my mind to go forward, to join those who hadn't been saved by Jesus. And all around me members of the congregation were quivering in what seemed like ecstasy, and the elderly man in front of me was uttering incomprehensible words that seemed to come from some mysterious inner depth.

But I resisted the compelling pull to declare myself unsaved by Jesus. Instead, I fought back my tears, and wished with all my might that the singing would end. When it did finally, I felt as if I'd just sat through one of those Hollywood tear-jerkers, a Spielberg weepie. But this hadn't been contrived. It'd been real, a genuinely spontaneous expression of a people's spiritual depths.

For the brief remainder of the service I sat there, feeling aggrieved that the issue of religious worship, which I thought I'd long settled, was in fact still unresolved. My religious education was minimal. I'd never been to a black church service. As a child, I attended a white church, Anglican or Methodist. I was never sure. My father used to insist that it was part of our education. But he himself never went. Our absence from the house on Sunday mornings gave him a chance to sleep in, when he wasn't working. Early in my teens, I rebelled against attending church on the grounds that it seemed to me that I was required to worship a pale-skinned, blue-eyed God. Perhaps if I'd attended a black church, I might still be practising some form of religion.

After the service, congregation members shook hands and hugged each other. The young man who'd been unable to contain his emotion and sobbed was comforted – and admired – by his friends and family. Several members approached me and shook my hand and called me "brother". It was all strange, but warm.

I learned later that I'd attended a Pentecostalist church. This denomination, which is widespread amongst Afro-

Caribbeans and Afro-Americans, does not worship graven images. This is perhaps part of its attraction to people of African descent. Individuals are free to see God in their own image.

An unforgettable moment in the service came when certain members of the congregation began speaking in tongues. The elderly man in front of me, for instance, uttered sounds, sometimes like gibberish, and at other times like a language. Speaking in tongues is apparently so common in black churches that only outsiders remark on it. I was quite intrigued, largely because it reminded me of a story I'd heard from a Nigerian friend. On a visit to Cuba he attended the rites of a religious cult. During the worship some members also began speaking in tongues, abandoning Spanish. My friend, a Yoruba, was shocked to hear Yoruba words in the mainly incomprehensible outpourings. He was even more shocked when he asked the worshippers if they knew what they'd been saying. None had any idea.

It's possible, then, that in those intensely emotional moments, people who speak in tongues are speaking another language. If so could it be an African language, a psychic retention from Africa? I am no linguist or psychologist. So an answer evades me. But the possibility of a psychic retention isn't as implausible as it may sound. Ali Mazrui, a famous Kenyan political scientist who has worked with Afro-Americans, has argued that the form of worship that many Afro-Americans engage in is rooted in African forms of worship. This includes the response and call acts, a feature unique to black churches. Says Mazrui: "There are in black services and black churches echoes of the sense of being possessed, reminiscent of many religious ceremonies in Africa. The spontaneous cries of Hallelujah are sometimes as persistent as the chanting in an exorcism ceremony in Africa."

The West Indies cricket team was playing in Australia. Defeat looked likely, and all over Handsworth elderly West Indians were lamenting their side's abysmal performance. One evening, in a Jamaican-run pub I overheard a conversation between the publican and two plain-clothes policemen. My companion, who claimed he could recognise a policeman anywhere, had pointed them out to me.

"Your boys are getting a right thrashing down under, George," said one of the cops.

"It's that bloody Australian surface," said the publican, his pride wounded. "Our boys've never liked their surface."

"I'll tell you what it is," said the other cop, grinning maliciously. "Your cap'n can't get any sensimilla, so he's 'ad to settle for black [Hashish]."

All three roared with laughter.

My companion was Phil Cooke, a Grenadian and West Indian in everything but his appearance. He defies racial categories. Spanish, Portuguese, Jewish, Scottish, Indian and African are included in his ancestry. He's a genuine New World man, a product of the Caribbean melting-pot.

He came to Britain in his late teens in the early Sixties. It was a move intended to quell his rebellious spirit. Driven to distraction by his penchant for trouble-making, his parents first sent him to Trinidad. He had an uncle in Port-au-Spain. But his uncle lost patience when Phil was caught throwing stones from a tree at soldiers in an American base. "Is something we used to do all the time, mahn," he told me. "An the soldiers them used to fire a few shots in the air. But that never frighten us. That's exactly why we threw the stones."

So Phil was sent back to Grenada. His parents then decided to send him here. On the way, his ship stopped in Lisbon. An anti-American demonstration was taking place and he joined in. He was arrested and deported to England. His "bad-man" behaviour continued in London. One night a policeman called him a Greek. He replied with a knife.

His keen eyes for detecting cops came from his numerous brushes with them. "In those days," he said, "these English cops didn't have any manners, mahn. Once you weren't white, they thought they could talk to you anyhow, call you any names they wanted to. We'd to put a stop to it, mahn." Even in jail he continued defying authority. Sentenced to solitary for a month for being involved in a fight, he did two hundred push-ups daily. When they released him he smiled at them with contempt. "I'd to show them they couldn't break me. That's what jail's about. Breaking you. Then they throw ya back out on the streets and expect you to be normal again. Mahn, this is one hypocritical system we live under."

Phil's law-defying days are over now. He's a property owner and occasional businessman. One of his past ventures involved leasing land from a Warwickshire farmer in order to grow Caribbean vegetables. But only the callaloo (a type of spinach) took to the soil. He abandoned the venture and has since concentrated on acquiring houses. Despite his violent past, he was a sensitive, warm person with a strong political conscience.

On Friday nights Phil's home became a venue for lively, raucous conversations. His friends came from all walks of life. And all had strong opinions, which they defended vigorously, but never without a sense of humour. One such night Phil, myself and Mark, a solicitor, were enjoying a bottle of rum in front of the television. An item on apartheid in South Africa interested us. Hollywood film distributors had announced their intention to join the apartheid boycott. They objected to segregated cinemas. The report included interviews with white South Africans. Asked if he favoured segregated cinemas, one man replied with a pained honesty: "That's the way it's always been. That's all we know." His agonised expression said it all.

Mark – muscular, gold-skinned, fiercely good-looking – sucked his cheeks in disgust.

"Whenever I see those white people in South Africa," said Mark, "I just get angry, mahn. Sometimes I just feel like boxing down the first white man ah see."

Phil grunted in agreement. "I don't know," I said, about to play devil's advocate. "That situation's pretty complicated. It's not just about black and white."

"I'm not dealing with rationality here," said Mark. "I'm telling you how I feel as a black man."

"So you can't be rational and be black man?" Phil asked teasingly.

"No, mahn. I'm not saying that. What I'm saying is South Africa makes me angry. All right, all right there's more to it than black and white. But doesn't stop you feeling a certain way when you see white cops shooting at unarmed black people, and licking them down with batons. When that country's free black people everywhere are gonna feel relieved."

"True," said Phil. "I suppose we all feel that way. That's why I've always reckoned that Botha's ban on news was an agreement between him and Britain. Remember the uprisings in '85. Before it happened, right through the summer, every day there was a report on South Africa. Some brutal pictures, mahn. It must've affected a lot of guys on the line."

"I thought the '85 riots were about the way the police were behaving in Handsworth," I said.

"Yeah, it was that, too," said Mark. "But imagine you getting licks here, and you see your brothers in South Africa getting worse licks and fighting back. You must join, mahn."

We were interrupted by the arrival of Gladstone, a middle-aged Jamaican. He was a carpenter and was carrying out repairs on one of Phil's properties. Without asking, he poured himself some rum, settled into a seat and began filling his pipe.

Mark resumed: "Anyway, we better be careful in this country. The way I see things going, the black community could be finished in ten or fifteen years' time."

An aromatic smell filled the room. George had lit his pipe and seemed to be listening with the supercilious air that a pipe can endow its user.

"Finished?" said Phil, "What do you mean finished?"

"Well, we're living under fascist government, mahn. You know how many black people in jail? Almost a third of the prison population is black."

"But Mark," Gladstone intervened, "don't you is a solicitor? How you can sit there and say that, me don't know. Is bad advertising, mahn. It means you guys not doing your job."

Phil and I laughed. But Mark didn't appreciate Gladstone's wit. He reacted angrily. He sprang up: "That's rubbish, mahn. Look, a fact that we were invited here to do these people's shit work. But there's over three million unemployed now. They don't need us any more. Now they're jailing us by thousands. Imagine what it does to a community when three hundred of its men are jailed. It's happened right here in Handsworth. Go down to Winson Green prison. You see for yourself. The next thing is repatriation."

"Well, all I know," said Gladstone, his face half-hidden by a cloud of smoke, "is that if I ever get in trouble with the law, me not coming to see you. No sah."

"You can't repatriate people who were born here," said Phil. "A heard the other day that well over half of the black population born here."

"Tell that to the Jews who ended up in Hitler's gas chambers," said Mark. "The same culture that produced Hitler is the same culture we living in."

Here, I reflected, was paranoia. Perhaps justifiable, but paranoia nonetheless.

"So you mean if I come to you with a legal problem, I might end up in a gas chamber," said Gladstone. "Well bwoy, one of my sons tell me de other day that 'im want to be a lawyer. Ah better advice 'im 'gainst it."

"Gladstone," said Mark firmly. "Why don't you climb up one of your ladders and dive off?"

Gladstone winked at me and smiled mischievously, and continued smoking his pipe. His wicked sense of humour had taken the steam out of Mark, who returned to his seat, defeat written across his face.

"I agree there's we have to be concerned," said Phil, "but I think the most dangerous thing at the moment is that state is creating a sort of black middle class. All those race relations advisers. They're there to police the community That's because black politics in this country has never had real direction. Our protests have never been about changing the system. We should be looking to build more alliances with the white working-class."

"The white working-class?" Mark said incredulously, "You got to be kidding Phil. That's the most racist part of the country, mahn. Them people is reactionary, conformist and have a history of betraying black people."

"They're our natural allies," said Phil, "if we're talking about socialism."

"That's just it," Mark retorted. "I'm not talking about socialism. I'm talking 'bout race first. Like Garvey said race must come first, mahn."

"Come on Mark," said Phil. "We living in Britain in 1987,

man, and where your argument leads to is segregation. Anyway, I don't see you involved in no kind of politics. All you do is talk it. And a lot of what you say don't make much sense."

We were now on our second bottle of rum. This probably accounted for what followed.

"I'm not involved in any politics," said Mark, "because all I want to see is destruction, all this white shit laid to waste. That's what I'm dealing with."

"I think there's more to it than that," Phil said. "Your ego's too big to be involved in politics."

"I wouldn't disagree there," Mark replied. "But tell you the truth, it's more than, too." He stood up and began walking up and down the room. "You see, gentlemen, I've got a number of, er, you might call perversions."

In *vino veritas*, Mark reached into his back pocket and pulled out two polaroid photographs. He studied them, then handed them to Gladstone. Gladstone's reaction was immediate – wild laughter.

"You see, I come very religious background. Repressive," said Mark. "When I broke away from it, I developed what you might call a hobby."

Gladstone passed the photographs to Phil, who also laughed on receiving them. And so did I when they reached me. They were pornographic pictures. Mark, a lawyer, walked around with pornographic pictures in his pockets.

He explained that he'd taken them himself. He always took pictures of his conquests. These were taken in an hotel in Greece while a pianist played below and the wind wafted in from the sea.

It was Phil who pointed out that they were disgusting. Gladstone was still laughing. When Phil asked how he'd feel to discover that one of girls in the picture was his daughter, a silence of shame seized him. Mark was by now regretting that he had brought out the pictures. He asked Phil if he could use his phone, and disappeared into another room.

It's strange how a serious incident can suddenly dispel the effect of alcohol, creating instant remorse, guilt. The evening continued at a more sedate pace after that. But some of Mark's sentiments, uttered under the influence of alcohol, I'd heard from sober lips.

It was Saturday night in the launderette and we were the only customers. He was what older Afro-Caribbeans would have described as a "red man". He wore a beige-coloured crombie coat, and had a pencil-thin moustache that seemed to accentuate his lugubrious face.

We got to talking when he asked me for a light. It's said that it's easier to unburden your troubles on a stranger. This is precisely what he did. Between long, almost desperate drags on his cigarette, he complained that his woman friend was giving him "a hard time". He suspected that she was having an affair with another man. Whenever he called on her, he swore, he could smell the interloper's scent.

"Every man have a scent," he said with scientific certainty. "And me know that scent in her house isn't mine. But me never catch her in the act, you see. This is the problem."

He ground his cigarette into the floor, and immediately lit another, sighed and said: "She's just a boogayaka, anyway." I'd never heard this word before, and had no idea what it could mean. He explained that it was a common person, someone lacking in decency.

"Is where you come from anyway," he asked, suddenly suspicious.

When I told him, he murmured sympathetically and said: "Must've come here young."

And that was how we began to talk about Jamaica and his migration to Britain.

Bosy was his name and he must have been in his early sixties, though he looked younger. His life story, told against the droning background noise of washing-machines and tumble-driers, disabused me of a number of common beliefs.

Bosy grew up in West Kingston, now called Denham Town. There he witnessed as a child a turbulent period in Jamaican history. He recalled often seeing Marcus Garvey walking down the street, and described him as a "squat, thick-neck man". When Haile Selassie was crowned Emperor of Ethiopia, the island was filled with excitement. Years later riots and demonstrations swept through Jamaica. Men took over street cars and everywhere defied authority.

"Sometimes," said Bosy, "you'd see a guy climbing up a statue of Queen Victoria and next thing you know, him just whip out a little steel hammer and lick off her head. Was a mad man, of course, but the crowd would cheer him, man. Another time a man might pull down the Union Jack and put up the red, gold and green."

But Jamaicans, he said, modelled themselves after the British. "Yes, honestly speaking," he said, seeing the surprise on my face. "They're a proud people. They were our masters and we copied them." Jamaicans, he insisted, radicalised black Americans. "You see, though we were under British rule, the island was ours. We weren't experiencing what the American Negro was going through. We didn't take that crap from whites, with them Jim Crow and all that."

Bosy recalled a Jamaican who'd been deported from Florida. He became a legendary figure in West Kingston. A migrant worker, the Jamaican took over a kitchen and renamed it "Friend's House", and cooked only Jamaican food. When the authorities chased him out, he retaliated by burning down the camp kitchen. "Dem didn't even bother try 'im," said Bosy. "Dem just export him."

Bosy was a young man in Kingston when Jamaicans began leaving for Britain in droves. He'd set his sights on the United States, but anti-immigration laws kept him out. "England wasn't de place for me, mahn. Everything was happening in de states."

When the history of Afro-Caribbean migration to Britain is told on television, one picture is often used. It shows the new arrivals disembarking from *The Empire Windrush*, and saying how glad they are to be in the mother country. Well, Bosy wasn't one of them. That wasn't his style of entry. Bosy began to change his mind about England when his friends who'd come here began to send him photographs. "Mahn, almost every month I get a picture of a friend in a sharp-looking zoot suit and standing next to a bad-looking car, you know gleaming thing." So Bosy stowed away to Britain. "Yes man, that's how me come here," he said proudly.

In Birmingham he met up with his friends. They were a small minority known as sporting boys. And they lived off their wits. Their days began with the dusk and ended with the dawn. Initially they haunted Birmingham night clubs. But the hostility from whites resulted in fights and many started walking with knives for protection. So they went where they pleased, properly armed, and whoever crossed them was left with scars for their abuses.

Bosy and his friends picked pockets, gambled, and imported ganja. "Used to get the t'ing with sugar, at the bottom, until customs guys caught on to it. One thing, I didn't do, though, was sell pussy. Easy money, mahn, 'cause them white gals love us up bad. We was exotic. They'd do anything for us. But it never seem right to me."

It was, claimed Bosy, people like him who started and ran blues dances.

"We couldn't go anywhere in those days, mahn, without one white man or another wanting a fight. And is not every time you go out in you' nice, nice suit that you want to have to cut up a man. So we started our own t'ing. A guy'd own a house with a basement and we'd rent the basement off him, bring in a sound system and we'd have a blues. It'd would last until the police found out. They'd close it down. But we'd just start another one somewhere else.

"We had some good times, mahn. Early morning we'd be going home and we'd see a group of breddas* going to work, we'd stop and give them a ride. People like us forge the way for guys who came later on. A man could go to work five, six days a week and know that come Saturday night or Friday night he's got somewhere to go without being hassled by no white people."

Bosy didn't understand the present generation. A man who took pride in his appearance, he declaimed their lack of style. "Mahn, we always, always look sharp. But these young guys, today, with them dreadlocks and t'ing?" He shook his head in despair.

Bosy recalled his early years in Birmingham with loving nostalgia. But he was getting old now. And he confessed that lately he'd been regretting his misspent youth. Many of those who came legitimately, and to work, were now in a position where they could return home. Several acquaintances and friends had gone back to Jamaica over the last ten years. They'd sold their houses and retired on the

*Brothers.

proceeds, along with their pension or redundancy payment.

"Mahn, few years back it seem like every Tom, Dick and Harry was going 'ome."

Though he was tired and yearning for Kingston, Bosy wasn't in a position to go home. He'd squandered every penny he'd made on rum, gambling, women and the blues dance. The party was over and he was trapped in Birmingham.

"Damn, woman," said Bosy wearily. "Time gone I'd just find myself another gal. But truth is me too tired, mahn. And you know something, I really love that woman."

6. Tiger Bay, Cardiff: A Rainbow Estate

Contrary to the timetable, there was no direct train to Cardiff that Sunday. A coach would ferry passengers to Gloucester. There we would connect with a Cardiff-bound train. The coach, of course, was late.

It was a bright and sunny day. Traces of spring danced in the weak sunlight. I found a sunspot and basked in its gentle warmth. Other passengers were less fortunate. With their luggage at their feet, they lined a wall like prisoners about to be executed, taking all their worldly possessions with them. An old Muslim Asian – his head covered by an ornate cap, his face leathery with wrinkles – approached me. He clutched a shoulder-bag and an Asian newspaper. His English was rudimentary. "Cardiff?" was all he said, pointing to the queue. I nodded and he shuffled away to stand beside a young white couple who were clinging to each other as if indissolubly welded together. A middle-aged white woman wearing an electric-blue coat came to stand beside me, her face set in a permanent scowl. The British Rail official paraded up and down, constantly looking at his watch and schedule-board. When he deigned to look at us, it was with the superior air of a prison warder.

The middle-aged woman became irate. She approached the official and demanded to know what had happened to the train, and what was happening to the coach, and why couldn't British rail get it right.

"I'd like to see you lot off as soon as possible," he replied. His tone was a mixture of pleading and impatience.

"My son's meeting me in Cardiff," she declared. "He won't wait all day."

"Madam," the official stated flatly. "We're doing our best."

"Your best!" she snorted. "Mrs Thatcher's got the right idea. Privatise the lot. That'll make things work better."

He looked at his watch, his schedule-board, then at her and said calmly: "Maybe, but I'll tell you what. There probably wouldn't be any kind of service to Cardiff on Sundays."

Touché, I thought, as the woman retreated, her scowl now made fiercer by the bitterness of defeat.

He was right. There were not enough passengers to justify a Sunday service in a profit-making railway. But I sympathised with the woman, too; especially as the sun was now retreating behind a bank of clouds, exposing me to the sharp afternoon air.

The coach arrived shortly and soon we were off. Once out of Birmingham, brown ploughed fields and green fallow land ran beside the motorway. The February sunlight created an electric effect, as if all beyond the window was unreal, a cinematic image.

As a boy I used to read about the verdant, undulating English countryside. But somehow I have never been able to appreciate it as an actuality. It remains something to be read about, to be seen in the cinema, on television. I have no rapport with it. I am an urban person, born in one city and brought up in another. There is an England of farmers and cottages and church-hall meetings and village greens that I will never know. A consequence of being an immigrant, a foreigner?

We had another long wait in Gloucester. I paced the platform and drank cups of so-called tea. The passing of a few local trains provided a little distraction from the boredom. Curious eyes would look at me from behind their glass cages, as if it were I, and not them, who were encased. I longed for the anonymity of the city again.

I'd never been to Wales and only realised that the train had crossed the border when it stopped. The passengers who embarked all spoke with a thick, guttural accent. The clarity of their diction, inexplicably, reminded me of Jamaican peasants. There was something simple and honest about their faces, too, like peasants, and I was struck by their varying shades, from pale white to a deep olive complexion. Yet all spoke in that sing-song Welsh-English. I dozed off and only woke up as the train was pulled into Cardiff station.

On my first morning in the South Wales capital I went in search of Tiger Bay. I caught a taxi from the station. The burly, unshaven driver was a man of few words. A few minutes later he stopped at the entrance to a council estate. It was all grey and there was not a tree in sight. Neither were there any people. I had no idea what Tiger Bay looked like, but I was convinced that this could not be it. I asked him to drive further. He dropped me at a junction, and, as I paid, he gave me a strange look.

I walked along a windy main road. The air was salty and I could hear the sea. Nearing a bridge I saw a black person for the first time. Hands in his raincoat pockets, he walked with his head bent low. I decided to ask him where Tiger Bay was. I stopped him. He was blue-black, with a gaunt face and sunken eyes. He looked like a North African, a Somali. He looked at me blankly, as if he hadn't understood. "Tiger Bay," I repeated. "Where do black people live round here?"

He spoke a stuttering English. I gathered he'd only been in Cardiff for three days. He could not help me.

Over the bridge, which spanned an inlet from the sea, I came upon another black person. He wore blue jeans and a battle-green fatigue jacket. I was optimistic. He directed me back to the junction where I'd been dropped. There I was to turn left until I came to a council estate. That was Tiger Bay. And that was how I discovered it.

Tiger Bay is officially known as Butetown. It is a council estate of less than a square mile. Its boundaries are so well-defined that once there, a visitor could quite easily forget where he is. On one side is a railway-line and canal. On the entrance side is the main road I'd been driven along, and beyond that an old dock wall, a high barrier of crumbling grey and black stones. A small commercial area serving Cardiff docks stands at one end; and at the other is Cardiff city centre.

Tiger Bay has much in common with Liverpool 8. Together they represent Britain's oldest settlement of people of African descent. Tiger Bay is not so old, though. It developed along with Cardiff Docks. From the second half of the nineteenth century, Cardiff was the paramount coal-exporting city in the world. Black sailors began arriving then, but their numbers really grew after the First World War.

Along with African and West Indian sailors, Tiger Bay also became home to Asians, southern Europeans, Filipinos and Chinese. In its heyday Tiger Bay was an exciting cosmopolitan community. An African sailor could easily find board and lodgings from a fellow African. Chinese opium-dens, night clubs and Arab-owned bazaars flourished.

It remains an incredible mixture of peoples from all over the world, a genuinely multi-cultural neighbourhood. Its most distinctive-looking inhabitants are Somalis. Dark, slim and usually tall, they are the only Tiger Bay residents who replenish their stock by bringing over their compatriots. Hence the Somali-looking man I met on my first day who couldn't speak English. Somalis are sometimes mistaken for Arabs, but they are quite distinct. They have their own mosque, built in the early 1970s. On Fridays it is filled with worshippers.

Another and older mosque is used by Arabs. Where exactly in the Arab world Butetown's Arabs originated wasn't easy to establish. But I did meet a Yemeni. He ran a cafeteria from the living-room of his council house. I was taken there one afternoon and received such a warm welcome and ate such a deliciously spicy meal that Wales seemed like another country far away.

Older residents still refer to the area as Tiger Bay. They can recall when everybody lived in Victorian and Edwardian houses originally built for ships' captains and their families. But few of these survive. Tiger Bay was a victim of the grand 1960s national redevelopment schemes. A solitary, characterless tower-block now casts its long shadow over faceless low-rise blocks and maisonettes. Whoever redesigned the redevelopment didn't consider trees or greenery as necessities. So Butetown, though clean, appears like a desolate concrete jungle. "They took the soul out of the place," an old resident told me. "Knocked down everything and erected these grey monsters. Mind you it was kind of overcrowded in the old days. But this . . ." she shook her head woefully.

Butetown has escaped the recent fate of several English inner-city neighbourhoods. In the riots of early Eighties, life continued apace. But it has known troubled times. Immediately after the First World War, Cardiff began to decline as the major coal-exporting port. As so often happens, economic decline brought in its wake racial hostility. Cardiff, like Liverpool, was the scene of serious disturbances in 1919. Several people, black and white, were killed. The riots are believed to have been sparked off by white men who resented seeing their women with African and West Indian sailors. A party of day-trippers – black men, their white wives and offspring, were attacked by a gang of whites. Weeks of shooting and killing followed (the frequency of such incidents in Black British history, I was told by a sociologist, is not simply due to racism. In primitive societies, the main sources of conflict between ethnic groups were economic ones and women).

For many decades after the 1919 riots, Tiger Bay had to carry the stigma of being a violent community – though its inhabitants had only been defending themselves. At one time, I was told by an eighty-year-old resident, the city council placed a sign on a bridge spanning the road leading into Tiger Bay. It read: "Whites and Europeans enter at their own risk."

The sign has been removed, but the stigma remains. Tiger Bay residents believe that other Cardiff folk see their neighbourhood as a den of evil, a place of vice and violence. And they are not mistaken. From *The South Wales Echo*:

> On Tuesday (S4, 9pm), the private detective played by Jeffrey Thomas is at it again amid the seedy surroundings of Cardiff's docklands; the pubs, the clubs, the pimps and the prostitutes.
>
> There are a series of brutal murders, where the victims are waylaid in their cars, armed robbery in a Cardiff street, an ice-cream van in the valleys peddling drugs to youngsters; an alcoholic Santa Claus involved in a child-kidnapping; a terrified wife and her young son seeking refuge from a brutal man; prostitutes dressed as nuns performing strange rituals based on a Celtic myth.

This article – headlined "Seedy sleaze on city underside" –

was a preview of a television series. Tiger Bay (or Butetown) is not mentioned, but everybody knows it is the only residential area around the docks. The series writer claimed that his episodes were based on real-life incidents. But by locating his protagonist in dockland he has reinforced Tiger Bay's largely mythical, unsavoury reputation.

Whatever Tiger Bay may have been in the past seems to have died, or is dying. Some of the African seamen who settled there are still alive. Now old and frail, they can sometimes be seen hobbling along the desolate streets at midday, on their way to the clinic or the shops. I met one on a bright, but cold afternoon. In that slow deliberate speech of the aged, he recalled the days when every sailor wanted to stop in Cardiff at least once. Its popularity amongst African sailors was surpassed only by that of Liverpool. He himself had heard about Tiger Bay while working as a stevedore in Freetown, Sierra Leone. "That," he concluded in a world-weary voice, "is how I come to be dying in this Tiger Bay."

He didn't have the time or the inclination to say much more. But another sailor was rather more forthcoming. He was simply called Mr Carey and we met in the local community centre. That we were both Jamaican and the warmth of the centre probably explain Mr Carey's volubility. He was a tall, distinguished-looking man, with a smooth brown complexion, and an implacably patient expression. As he spoke he twirled his walking-stick.

Mr Carey had lived in Cardiff since the late Thirties. He ended up there after falling out with his wealthy Jamaican family. His father objected to his friendship with the family chauffeur. "Foolish man," said Mr Carey. "'Cause a man drive your car don't mean you can't drink with him." It was his refusal to observe the island's class distinctions which eventually forced his flight to Canada, then Wales. Despite Tiger Bay's recent troubled past he grew, and remains, fond of it. "Take my word," he insisted. "A Welshman is much friendlier than the Englishman. I never meet no prejudice in Wales. But England and the English! Lawd gawd everytime me see a Englishman, me think of the devil."

My conversation with Mr Carey was my first proper introduction to Welsh nationalism. Of course I'd seen the public signs which are written in Welsh as well as English, and I'd heard of Welsh nationalists using violence to achieve their goals. But I'd never met a Jamaican who made such a sharp distinction between Britons. Mr Carey, I guess, has to be described as a Jamaican-Welsh nationalist.

Living, as I do, in London, a capital city that affords one of the best vistas on to the world, it is dangerously easy to overlook the significance of the sub-nations that make up Great Britain. But British national unity is neither a stable nor an immutable entity. The occupation of Northern Ireland by British troops – and the resentment that fuels amongst Irish nationalists – is a violent reminder of Britain's underlying fragility as a nation state. My brief stay in Wales made me realise that other fissures could one day assume great importance.

By sheer coincidence, the same day I met Mr Carey, the Jamaican-Welsh nationalist, I read the following reader's letter in *The South Wales Echo*:

Wales the nation is a colony, this is incontrovertible. "The rose I wear is the rose of England," said Mrs Thatcher. Britain means England.

The law and the constitution itself are English. The memorable Macaulay wrote about English history, as does the benign Professor Asa Briggs. The latter confirms that "Wales has her own history".

Let us have a real United Kingdom, yes, but recognition of the Welsh and Scottish nations within that can only invigorate and strengthen the whole, given the will and the wisdom. Anything less will surely lead to fragmentation and utter decline.

Finally, devolved political power is a necessary condition of economic balance and health. That is true even of England's "two nations", much less a Wales where all we have known is economic deprivation.

I found this letter fascinating. It had always intrigued me how a nation as small as Britain could colonise over half the world. Part of the answer must lie in the English state's successful colonisation and incorporation of its ethnic neighbours, the Welsh and the Scottish. But the process of unification, the birth of Britain, was swiftly followed by imperial exploits. All ethnic groups, but the English more so, benefited. And up until the Second World War Britain could satisfy the demands of its sub-nations from the proceeds of Empire.

Could it be, then, that in the absence of Empire, with all its endless military campaigns, as well as lucrative material rewards, the sub-nations will begin to re-assert themselves? Wales and Scotland rejected devolution in the 1970s. But, as the Empire becomes nothing more than a glorious memory, it is possible that regional nationalism will become an increasingly important political factor.

Unfortunately for the people of Tiger Bay, Welsh nationalism is ambivalent towards them. While the Welsh continue their centuries-old battle for national assertion, its people of

African descent sometimes feel like a neglected minority, so much flotsam and jetsam washed up by the receding tides of prosperity.

Similar sentiments prevail in England. An important difference, though, is that Tiger Bay residents didn't exhibit the same bitter anger towards whites outside their neighbourhood as, for instance, their Liverpool counterparts. Incidents of racial abuse and insults were recounted to me with much good humour.

Sarah Taylor is a pensioner who was born in Tiger Bay. Her mother was Welsh and father Liberian. In the Second World War, she worked in an munitions factory. Later she married a black American soldier (Afro-Americans are still highly prized catches for Tiger Bay women. I was told that on the rare occasions when an American ship docks in Cardiff, mothers encourage their daughters to go fishing for potential rescuers from Tiger Bay's grim reality).

Sarah recalled that as a child she and her mother often met with racial abuse beyond Tiger Bay. Her mother, because she'd married an African, lost her status as a white person. Not, it appeared, that Sarah's mother was unduly worried. In fact, she sounded as if she must have been a redoubtable woman. In one incident, Sarah told me, her mother actually bared her backside to a group of men and women who'd been abusing her.

Sadly, some of yesterday's incidents are still being replayed today. Steve Kayira, whose parents are Somali, told me of one which had happened the previous evening. He and his friends had gone along to a football match – Wales versus the Soviet Union. Naturally, they supported Wales. But their evening was spoilt by a white gang of fellow supporters who took great pleasure in chasing them after the match. But Steve related the episode as one would a school-yard fracas.

He simply dismissed the gang as hooligans, and boasted that "they wouldn't dare set foot in Tiger Bay". It was a revealing remark. It seems that the community's past record of having successfully defended itself has left a legacy of pride that enables them to cope with outsiders who make an issue out of the colour of their skins.

Another source of pride for Tiger Bay residents must be the fact that it is a genuinely multi-racial, multi-cultural community. People seem to take great delight in explaining their genealogy. Decades of intermarriage between Africans, Filipinos, Europeans, Asians, Chinese and Arabs have left many people with features that defy common racial categories. One multi-limbed Tiger Bay family traces its origins back to 1919, and marriage between a St Kitts seaman, Joseph Dixon, and a Bristol woman, Emily Ashford. The couple fled to Wales after threats from the bride's family. They lived in a Welsh valley originally, but when Joseph Dixon died, his wife married a Sierra Leonean seaman and moved to Tiger Bay. Today, the family numbers over one hundred members. "The Rainbow Family", a national newspaper dubbed them. It's an apt description. They represent a range of subtle shades and features between Africans and Europeans.

Tiger Bay's melting-pot history can be embarrassingly confusing to an outsider. Some people who appear white turn out to have African or Afro-Caribbean ancestors. And some are quick to let you know that they regard themselves as being black.

This was the case with Keith Gittens. I was introduced to him in a pub, and there was absolutely nothing in his features intimating that he might be anything other than a full-blooded Welshman. Later in the evening I learned that his father came from St Lucia in the Caribbean. He had written a poem to his father and insisted on reciting it to me. It was called "My proud West Indian father" and evoked images and sentiments which I, as a Jamaican, could identify with. And it was eerie, listening to someone who was physically white, but whose words and emotions seemed to originate from the same source as mine.

Keith's life was complicated. He had moved out of Tiger Bay, but retained a strong sentimental attachment to the area. There he was known and had many childhood friends. "It's the only place I feel really relaxed in," he said. Beyond the bridge that marks Tiger Bay's boundary, his life is filled with uncertainties. His white complexion enables him to secure jobs which his darker friends stand no chance of getting; but he feels lonely. Sometimes he finds himself in the company of whites who unwittingly reveal their bigotry. He'd got into more than one fight in such a situation.

He told me of other people like himself who pass as white but who also live tormented lives: like his friend whose complexion enabled him to secure a much sought-after job on the docks. He stuck it for three weeks, then walked out when he couldn't take the canteen conversations about his people.

"It's not easy," said Keith. "Nobody in their right mind would stay in Tiger Bay. But once you leave, you learn there's a world out there where black and white really matter, are all that matters to some people."

Tiger Bay represents the most likely long-term future for most of Britain's black communities: intermarriage with whites, a gradual whitening, with those light enough drifting off into white society, though not without discomfort. For those unable to pass for white, social isolation and hostility.

★

Cardiff is being transformed into one of Britain's water cities. Similar redevelopments have been completed, or are being completed in many former British ports. The most famous is the docklands in London. The oldest parts of Cardiff docks have been demolished and an opera house, civic centre, residential dwellings and offices are being built around a disused marina. The redevelopment site is separated from Butetown by Bute Road and the old dock wall. When it is completed Cardiff's new face will look away from Tiger Bay, as if in shame. The dock wall will be heightened, and landscaped green banks built – both will obscure Butetown's view of the rejuvenated dockland.

As in London's docklands, the people who live closest to the redevelopment will gain the least. It promises employment for Butetown's residents. But few people take this possibility seriously. "Employment," a young resident scoffed. "You mean working in thar kitchens and cleaning thar offices." He wasn't far wrong. Certainly, the luxury houses planned will be beyond the means of most people in Tiger Bay, Cardiff's highest area of unemployment.

The redevelopment is an issue over which tempers run high. People feel cheated, insulted, walked over. Their resentments were not new to me. As a reporter on a London magazine, I'd covered several stories in the London docklands area. One incident involved a mysterious fire. It razed ten luxury chalets which had been interposed between a council block and a marina, obscuring the council tenants' view of the water. Their parents' grandparents had worked on the docks and, rightly or wrongly, they believed it was their legacy. The fire had been started deliberately, but the arsonist was never caught. The community closed its ranks to the investigators. It was a classic instance of the victims of progress retaliating with the only weapon they had:

destruction. Development from above breeds discontent below.

The inhabitants of Tiger Bay had not yet gone to that extreme. But their angry condemnation of the redevelopment suggested that political vandalism was an imminent possibility.

I took a stroll over the redevelopment site one afternoon. Skeleton structures had been erected and roads marked out or half-constructed. Next to each building site, encircled by wire fences, were the portable offices of the construction companies. Men in bright steel helmets, donkey jackets and wellington boots busied themselves over blueprints. Resounding hammer blows, the incandescent sparks of electronic welding machines, truck engines straining under heavy loads of earth or building materials – all promises of a rejuvenation intended to take Cardiff into the twenty-first century.

The Marina is about the size of a football pitch. Its water was dark-green and opaque and a cold wind blew off it. At one end, where a canal began, fishermen of various ages and colour sat patiently, their heads lowered, staring into the water. A few hundred yards from them builders were clambering over a Victorian warehouse. Its brickwork had been cleaned and new windows installed. Along the canal bank another warehouse, as yet untouched, stood forlornly, its walls covered in dark-green grime, its windows dark cavities. Decades must have passed since it was last used.

And it seemed a shame that a theoretically good idea should arouse such bitterness. The people of Tiger Bay had lived with these ruins all their lives. I imagined it must have been a wonderful, if sometimes dangerous, adventure-playground. Soon it would be off-limits to them, invaded by office-workers, opera-goers and day-trippers with money to spend. Perhaps a few intrepid voyeurs would wander into Tiger Bay. But on the whole the two worlds would never meet. And Tiger Bay would be left in its grey isolation.

Some people, though, who have taken a pragmatic approach to the growth of Cardiff's water city are the United Children of Israel. They are a group of Rastas who, amongst other things, run a video and film workshop. I met them whilst they were filming the redevelopment site. They were committed to documenting its construction and local reactions. They reminded me of Gaddafi and the Frontline Posse. None had had a formal education beyond school. But through determination and perseverance, they had managed to attract funding for their project. They even had a few minor film credits to their name.

After our initial meeting, wherever I went in Tiger Bay I ran into a member of the United Children of Israel. With their huge leather caps and red, gold and green shoe-laces, there was something comically Neanderthal about them. But they were a serious bunch and sometimes made interesting conversation.

It was one of the Rastas who brought up an issue which I'd been thinking about since Birmingham. We were talking about going back to Africa, when one of them said: "We'll get there, we know we will. After all, centuries ago we were called slaves, then Negroes, then coloureds, then black, and now we call ourselves Africans. To go back physically, we have to first do it spiritually."

His romanticism apart, he'd broached an issue of some significance. The language used to describe people of African descent is a linguistic minefield. What is being signified when a person is described as black? In the 1960s Afro-Americans insisted on the right to define themselves as black. The Portuguese noun Negro became offensive. But then to call oneself black, as opposed to coloured or Negro, implied political radicalism. Today the term has no such connotation. In fact, it has almost become synonymous with "non-white immigrants". Asians, Chinese and people of African descent are all black. When a word embraces such a diversity of peoples it is surely meaningless. It neither signifies where they originate from in the world nor their colour. Except, of course, that they are not of European origin. Even used exclusively, in relation to people of African descent the term black has little meaning, especially in communities like Tiger Bay where people are a fantastic range of shades and features.

I saw a striking example of contrasting shades one evening in the Tiger Bay community centre. I'd gone there hoping to watch a local drum and dance group in rehearsal. Instead, I met a slim youth with long, dark wavy hair that was pulled backwards and held together by a red, gold and green band. He was like a living picture of an ancient Greek youth. In that empty hall he played criss-cross rhythms on a Ghanaian drum and cow horn. He was later joined by a rakishly thin, extraordinarily dark and beautiful youth who looked as if he had stepped out of a North African desert. He was a Somali, and the first boy of a mixture of races which I could not begin to identify.

So perhaps the Rasta was right. It would be more accurate to refer to them as Afro-Britons. For it was their African heritage that they most had in common. It was not their colour. Even some full-blooded Welsh I saw were darker than some Tiger Bay residents.

The Rastas introduced me to an Afro-American anthropologist who was carrying out research on Tiger Bay. His name was Glen Jordan and he came from California. His doctoral supervisor was St Clair Drake, who had, in the 1940s, also studied Tiger Bay. Glen was following up his research. We struck up an immediate friendship. Within hours of our introduction he offered to put me up while I was in Tiger Bay. I accepted gladly, mindful of my mounting hotel expenses.

Later on Glen's scholarly detachment helped me to recover from an unpleasant experience in Cardiff Docks. On my way to the docks, a van load of white workers shouted at me: "Right nigger." It was broad daylight, and I was less than five minutes' walk from Butetown. It was years since I'd been so addressed. I continued on my way in a state of agitation. It subsided when I viewed the shimmering, silvery sea and heard the gentle music created by the sound of anchor chains knocking together in the inexhaustibly restless sea. When I got back to the house, I related the incident to Glen. Had he had a similar experience in Cardiff? "No," he replied, looking down at me over the rim of his glasses. He was tall. "What can I say?" he continued. "I am here as an anthropologist, man. If I was here as a black vigilante, I'd say let's go get those motherfuckers."

I had to laugh. With that laughter I felt more at ease. Later that evening I recalled that in Nigeria children are in the habit of calling whites Oyinbo (Yoruba) or Bature (Hausa). Neither word has any abusive connotations. Literally translated, they mean strangers. The point, though, is that it was a practice of children. Peasants in the remotest bush use Oyinbo or Bature to any outsider. My irritation was finally quashed when I could see the men who had abused me as children, or adults of limited mental growth.

7. Bristol: The Children of Scipio Africanus

I had made enquiries about travelling to Bristol across the Severn. But few Tiger Bay residents knew if it would be possible. It was a retired Welsh sailor who informed me that such a crossing would be dangerous at this time of year. Few boats made the journey. Anxious to get away I settled for a more mundane form of transport – bus.

As I left, I realised that I'd seen little of Cardiff. I'd unwittingly fallen prey to Tiger Bay's charming insularity. It had completely absorbed me for ten days. Through the coach windows, I could see in the distance the Welsh valleys begin: great sweeps of verdant glacial land. I reflected that next time, if there was a next time, I would endeavour to see more of Cardiff and Wales.

Once I'd lost sight of the valleys the scenery became familiar. A road sign told me I was back in England. Soon the rooftops, spires, and stadium lights of Bristol appeared. I was surprised how close I'd been to the English city.

The taxi-driver frowned when I asked if there was a hotel near St Paul's. His reply was an abrupt "No". I sensed that he was not a talker, and asked to be dropped at a reasonably priced hotel. He grunted, and that was the extent of our conversation.

The taxi-driver's reticence, I later learned, was probably due to the mention of St Paul's. For later that day I discovered that Bristol is extremely uncomfortable with its Afro-Caribbean population. I'd never been to Bristol before, so I was relying on a taxi to drop me in St Paul's. The driver of the first taxi I flagged down would not do it.

"A few of our cars have been waylaid in there," he said warily.

"Waylaid!" I exclaimed, being unfamiliar with this rather archaic-sounding expression.

"You know, held up. Drivers were badly beaten up, too."

He was a middle-aged man, probably a husband, a father, and he was deadly serious.

I was stunned, but recovered quickly enough to suggest he drop me off on a main road near or running through St Paul's.

He agreed. On the way he volunteered that not everybody in St Paul's had to be feared. An unruly minority were responsible for the area's poor reputation: those on drugs. "Some of the hardest working people I know are West Indians," he said, looking at me through his rear-view mirror, "But some of those youngsters, well. . . ."

He did not finish his sentence. It was not necessary.

He stopped on a narrow main road and said, "Right. This's it." I paid, got out, and watched as he executed a U-turn before speeding off.

The taxi-driver appeared to have exaggerated. The area had a Sunday afternoon calm. Only a few people were on the street. A Jamaican café provided me with a long-desired meal of rice and peas and chicken. I felt very much at home. From my seat near the window I saw a group of youths pass by. One carried a ghetto-blaster. Its music lingered in the air long after they'd passed.

It was some days later before I went back into St Paul's. Bristol is an old city, and its many narrow cobbled streets were a fascinating maze of history. Everywhere I went in central Bristol I discovered centuries-old buildings. One morning I found a church that dated back to the fourteenth century; on another day an eighteenth-century almshouse. Bristol, I realised, is also the model for the water cities emerging throughout Britain. Built on an estuary of the Avon, which winds its way around the city, it has in parts, an atmosphere similar to Amsterdam. Office-blocks and restored warehouses hug the banks. And from my room in the Unicorn Hotel I could see the leisure area with its boat rides, boat restaurants, museums, an art gallery and a craft market. After ten days in the grey monotony of Tiger Bay, I was glad to be in what seemed like a cultured artistic city.

Bristol's preserved antiquity and maritime distractions were all new to me. It was by far the most beautiful city on my journey. And it is one of those British cities whose name constantly recurs in history books on the West Indies. In the early part of the eighteenth century, it was second only to London in its involvement in the Atlantic slave trade. And up until the mid-nineteenth century, its shipping links with the West Indies were crucial to the city's prosperity. Like Liverpool, Bristol is an old slave port. In fact, centuries before the Atlantic slave trade, Bristol merchants dealt in white slaves. Some of its street names reflect its African connections. There is, for instance, Black Boy Hill. So named, I am told, because that was the place where African page-boys, favoured by the fashion-conscious wives of the city's eighteenth-century ship-owners, were left by their mistresses when visiting town. In the same neighbourhood is Whiteladies Road.

Bristol also has one of the oldest graves of an African in Britain. The name inscribed on the tombstone is Scipio Africanus, and it is dated 1720. His epitaph reads:

Bristol: The Children of Scipio Africanus

I who was born a pagan and a slave,
Now sweetly sleep a Christian in my grave.
What tho' my hue was dark my savior's sight
Shall call this darkness into radiant light.
Such grace to me my Lord on earth has given
To recommend me to my Lord in Heaven
Whose second coming here I wait
With Saints and angels him to celebrate.

Scipio Africanus was probably born somewhere in West Africa. And despite his epitaph, no doubt composed by his master, I am inclined to think that if his spirit went anywhere, it was back to Africa, to the company of the gods there.

But the fact that one can find so much evidence of Bristol's slave past distances it from Liverpool. I left Liverpool thinking that it was a city ashamed of its past, repressing it, attempting to obliterate it from memory. One gets no such impression in Bristol. Inevitably, in a city so old, there is no shortage of museums. I spent a morning in the largest – the City Museum and Art Gallery. It has amongst its exhibits a minor collection of loot seized during the punitive British military expedition to Benin of 1897, which was in retaliation for the killing of Royal appointed traders. There is also a fine collection of Ashanti gold weights.

The museum also houses a collection of eighteenth-century prints of life in Bristol. Two depict families with African male servants. Always the Africans appear to be lovingly caring for young children. Confronted by these images, I wondered what it was really like for these servants. How did they live? What were their lives like outside work? Did they have lovers? Did they long for the heat of the African sun, and the warm company of their fellow tribesmen?

Wandering around the museum I came across a most

163

unusual painting. So far all the images of Africans I'd seen depicted servility, the letters slavery, and the artefacts colonial subjugation. This picture was radically different. It is called "The Combat". A handsome, muscular coffee-coloured African sat astride a white horse. He was naked but for a loin-cloth, and held a spear. The horse's expression was one of terror. A fierce lion was slashing at it. The rider and his steed were under attack from this wild, savage creature. The artist is obscure, Alfred Dedereux, and it might have been painted around the 1850s. It was open to any possible number of interpretations. The first thought it prompted was that the white horse represented Europe, and the African's attempt to master that continent's civilisation. But ... explain the lion. The lion could be seen as the ... gery of the African continent. So African and ... n were united in their battle against a continent ... has been described as the world's most inhospitable ... ronment. There is another equally plausible interpreta-on. The lion by the 1850s had become a symbol of the British Empire. The artist's name is French and France, with Germany, is historically Britain's greatest rival. Is the artist, then, using the white horse to symbolise France? Possibly. The French and the African united against the British Lion.

The painting was pregnant with meaning, and would linger in my mind for some time. Not simply because of its possible symbolism, but because it was the only old European image that I saw on my journey, which depicted an African with valour, dignity and strength.

On the same floor of the museum was a temporary exhibition on Bristol's Caribbean connection. It was disappointing in size, but revealing in its contents. A glass case contained a number of letters with various Caribbean islands, mainly Barbados and Jamaica. One, dated 1760, from an agent in Jamaica, informed an employer that "rebellions of the negroes are causing a shortage of salt beef and other goods on the island". Another one was a moving appeal from a Barbadian slave plantation overseer. It deferentially requested that the absentee plantation owner grant the overseer's offspring from a liaison with a slave the status of a free person. Unfortunately, there was no reply. One was left to speculate on the outcome of the overseer's request. Maybe almost two centuries later, the overseer's illegitimate descendants were amongst the thousands of Afro-Caribbean immigrants who settled in Bristol.

They were not greeted with open arms. St Paul's, Bristol's present Caribbean connection, is a model of post-Second World War black settlement in Britain. From the early Fifties, white Bristolians began moving out of the area's larger houses. Their departure coincided with the arrival of Afro-Caribbeans. Accommodation was the first hurdle that the newly-arrived had to face. Whites in most parts of Bristol closed their doors to them. St Paul's was the only area where they could find digs. When white Bristolians looked up and noticed that the neighbourhood was run down, they blamed the immigrants.

The newly-arrived were able to secure lowly paid work in and around Bristol. But their social life was restricted to St Paul's, where six or seven grown men would be living in one room. And, even here, they only went out at night in large groups. At local dances their advances to white women provoked jealousy in white men. Fights were common. Teddy Boys used St Paul's as a hunting ground for the Caribbeans.

As late as 1963 Bristol's bus corporation operated a "colour bar". Collusion between workers and management ensured that no Afro-Caribbeans were employed as drivers or conductors. A four-month bus boycott by Afro-Caribbeans (inspired by Afro-American protests) finally ended the "colour bar". It was an acrimonious affair which implicated the city's leading trade union figures and the city fathers in racist practices. In those days, though, the milder "colour prejudice" was the norm.

Some of the earliest Afro-Caribbean settlers in Bristol were former soldiers. They were mainly Jamaicans, men who had fought for King and country, for the mother country, in the Second World War. The ex-servicemen are the elders of Bristol's Afro-Caribbean community. These old soldiers, who are slowly fading away, can recount their early years – the hostility they met at the hands of citizens of a country they'd risked their lives to defend, the prejudice they encountered trying to secure accommodation; but also the friendliness of some Bristolians, especially women, without whom their lives would have been intolerable. Not all of those who fought for the mother country did so voluntarily. Lloyd Brown is a sternfaced Jamaican whom I met through Bristol's West Indian Association. We spoke in the living-room of his St Paul's house. Now in his late sixties, Lloyd was an apprentice mechanic in Jamaica when the war broke out. One day his employer called him and the other apprentices together and told them that as they were all young they should volunteer. If they refused, they would be dismissed. Lloyd then, was a reluctant soldier. But once he'd joined up he didn't shirk his duties. His transport ship was torpedoed twice between Canada and Britain. And he fought in Sicily and Algeria, and spent three months in Germany immediately after the war.

It was in Sicily that Lloyd Brown realised what the war was about: defence of the mother country. "They talk about democracy and all that," he said dismissively, "but really it was all about stopping Hitler from getting his greedy hands on England and her colonies. There was nothing in it for people like me. I mean, I reach that conclusion after some hard thinking, man. It was a white man's war. I didn't have a choice but fight. But ah say to myself, I not dying in this war. You know what that America general said, 'The purpose of war is to stay alive and kill as many of the next dumb bastards on the other side.' That was my attitude. Me didn't even bother too much 'bout killing another man, just staying alive, man."

When the war ended Lloyd Brown found himself in another battle–field. His regiment was stationed in Filey, Yorkshire, awaiting demob orders. Friction between Jamaicans and Barbadians was a daily occurrence. A senior officer who "understood Jamaicans" separated the two. "You see," Lloyd explained, "the Bajan is a man more loyal to the flag than the British themselves. Jamaicans kinda different." He did not say what the difference was, and I did not press him. Our conversation proceeded as if there was tacit understanding and acceptance of the differences between the two islands.

The conflict between Afro-Caribbeans was soon overshadowed by a more serious rivalry. British soldiers were returning. They "were coming back with nothing and to nothing. It caused a lot of jealousy. Things got rough." Canadian, Australian and New Zealand troops supported the Afro-Caribbeans. "They'd come on our side. The British didn't like nobody but themselves. They're a selfish lot of buggers." But he stressed that the Jamaicans relied as much as possible on their own resources for defence. "That's how you see Jamaicans start walk with knives. You see, all over we're a people who don't stand for nonsense. We help ourselves. So when they start attack us, we cut them with knives."

Before the British troops returned, Lloyd Brown had befriended a local Yorkshire family. "Everything was rationed then. The soldiers used to get more than the civilians. I used to bring what I could to this friend. Me and 'im got on well. So I'd sneak out food for him and his family. They were always hungry, see. So one day, this chap I am seeing as my friend, white chap, says to me, 'Lloyd, why don't you go home seein as the war is over.' You know, I walk out of that man's house, and I never go back there again, never. Damn feisty 'bout why don't I go home."

I was initially puzzled at this part of Lloyd's story. But later I realised the cause of his indignation. He'd been torpedoed in the Atlantic, shot at in Sicily, dug graves for corpses in Germany – all for Britain, the country, which as a Jamaican he would have grown up believing was the mother country. He may have only arrived in the war, but it was as much his home as Jamaica.

The fighting began to abate as the soldiers were demobbed. But it only ended when a white civilian was killed. Lloyd and his friends travelled across the Pennines to Manchester one night. A fight between the Afro-Caribbean soldiers and local men broke out, resulting in the death of one of the latter. The incident was national news. A member of the party was mistakenly picked out as a scapegoat. "They pick the wrong man," said Lloyd. "This guy wouldn't hurt a fly. Nobody really knew who did it. It was a messy brawl." The accused was acquitted with the help of a famous Jamaican lawyer, flown over for the case – Norman Washington Manley, later to become Jamaica's prime minister.

In 1947 Lloyd Brown went home for the first time in five years. But there was no work. America's doors were still open to the West Indies then, and he worked there for a year and a half, before returning to Britain in 1957. By now he was married with two children, and like a true West Indian colonial, he wanted his children to have the benefit of a British education.

He settled in St Paul's because a few old friends were living there. In those days there were only three Afro-Caribbean owned houses. But through an informal saving system popularly known as 'pardner hand' – or 'sous-sous' to other islanders – he and many others were able to buy houses.

When his son reached sixteen Lloyd tried to get him an apprenticeship. It was not easy. "Mahn, that was a job in itself," he said emphatically. "They had a man down at the labour exchange who every time I bring my son there was saying we should come back another time. One day I got there when he wasn't there, and his secretary say to me, 'Mr Brown, my boss will never give your son a job. He's colour-prejudiced.' So the next day I go back and I confront, yes, I look him straight in the eyes and I tell him he's a 'colour-bar man', and I told him he wouldn't see me in there again."

Lloyd Brown did finally get his son a job, through the help of another white. He stuck it for a year, went to night classes, and got the necessary qualifications to enter university. After university he went straight back to Jamaica, where he is now in a secure and well-paid job. "I can tell you," said Lloyd, "I was relieved to see him go, 'cause he wouldn't have got the job he wanted, even with 'is qualifications. Not in this country."

Lloyd Brown retired from the railway in 1984. As our interview came to a close, he walked over to a cabinet and said, "Wait a minute". From the cabinet he produced a case which contained two medals, his service medal from the war, and a medal from British Rail for working on the new express inter-city trains which were launched in Bristol's Temple Meads station. He was proud of his medals. But I could not reconcile his pride with the bitterness with which he spoke about his early years in Britain. I sensed in him a man wounded by that experience.

A less angry old soldier was Bill Smith. He also came from Jamaica, and a wager with his friends led to his recruitment into the army. After six weeks' recruitment training in Jamaica he was flown over to Filey.

"Bristol has been good to me," Bill Smith told me. A retired Justice of the Peace, he lived in a comfortable corner terraced house in a working-class area neighbouring St Paul's. His wife was English, and their two daughters had married English men. "That's just the way it happened," he said without prompting, perhaps embarrassed. "Important thing's they're happy."

Bill Smith and Lloyd Brown may have had different experiences of Britain, but they had in common a bewilderment at the younger generation. Lloyd Brown had told me that he had warned his daughter's children that, if they even joined the Rastafarians, they wouldn't be allowed in his house. Bill Smith's sentiments were less harsh, but similar. "When I was a young man," he said, "Rastafari were an outcast section of the society. We were brought up to see England as the mother country. On the King's birthday, at school we sang the patriotic songs, like 'Britons never will be slaves'. I was born British. This talk of going back to Ethiopia seems meaningless to me. They can't afford to look after themselves. It's not the sort of place I'd be wanting to run to."

His criticisms of the Rastas were measured, as one would expect from a former JP. His strongest objection to them was their use of ganja. "People use it in Jamaica as tea, but it's still a legal offence. I don't know the second generation. There's third generation, too. I know them even less."

An ex-serviceman who seemed more tolerant of the present generation was Earl Shakespeare. He hailed from Port Royal in Jamaica and joined the British merchant navy in the Second World War. His father had served in the First World War. He lived on City Road, in the heart of St Paul's. While the first two old soldiers were respectable sorts, Earl Shakespeare was a bohemian. His friends were mainly drawn from St Paul's hippy community. The flower children, I learned from Bristol, did not collectively overdose. They are highly visible in St Paul's. One night I was overtaken by a blonde girl with flowers in her hair and bells on her ankles. And she was barefoot, despite it being early March.

Earl Shakespeare shared Bill Smith's thoughtfulness. Although he was in his late fifties, he was an aspiring actor and musician. And he had some evocative descriptions of the Jamaica he once knew. "In Port Royal, man, you could watch the sun set over the sea. It would create golden, luminous path that seemed almost real, like you could walk on it. In the mornings you would wake up and catch shrimps and lobsters while across the harbour Kingston would still be sleeping."

He was a dark, unshaven, untidy man who seemed to occupy a world of his own. His flat was sparsely furnished. The walls were bare, but for a photographic display above the gas fire. One of the first questions he asked me was whether I noticed anything unusual about the pictures. I couldn't. So he explained that all the pictures depicted him doing different things: in one he was dressed in a military uniform, a part in a movie; in another he played drums in a band, others showed him with friends. I had not recognised that they were all of the same person. "Sometimes, mahn," he said grinning, "I just sit down here and stare at those pictures for hours, trying to work out how one man, one human being, could have so many faces. You think it's gift or a curse?"

"Maybe it's both," I said without commitment.

"You know that's why I haven't married. I have this fear that my wife would wake up one morning and not recognise me and start screaming how she wake up with a stranger. I mean, I even scare me sometimes."

The ex-servicemen have been pushed into the shadows by the new and angry generation. They were mainly born here or brought to Bristol as very young children. They were both the descendants of the Scipio Africanus and the white plantation overseer. And they see little value in the culture of their former masters. The idea of Britain being some sort of mother country – which brought their parents and grand-parents here – is complete anathema to them.

St Paul's has a similar atmosphere to Handsworth. But because it is smaller, trends which are vague elsewhere are crystallised. The urge for Africa – which I mentioned before – is given its most advanced expression in St Paul's. Certain graffiti recur around St Paul's – "Garveyism" and "Back to Africa". Posters in shop and house windows declare the neighbourhood an anti-apartheid free zone. The red, gold and green is, of course, ubiquitous. On one house, it is a sheet-size flag that flutters and dances in the March wind. In a central spot, a maxim popularised by an Afro-American group, the Last Poets, declares: "Niggers are scared of revolution."

The area bristles and crackles with tension, pent-up energy, and a creativity crying out for recognition. Police-men only walk in twos along St Paul's' dirty streets of dilapidated houses. And they seem for ever poised to call in reinforcements. The centre of St Paul's begins where City Road meets Grosvenor Road. A small, patchy green accentuates rather than beautifies the area's raggedness. Recently-built council blocks contrast with blackened, eyeless buildings. The largest houses, made from Bath stone, are the saddest looking. Colour is provided by a new bookshop, The Hummingbird, which is sited close to a record shop which also sells Rasta paraphernalia and African carvings. Further along, across the road, is a Jamaican-owned pub. Next door to that is a Jamaican café-cum-restaurant.

It was in there one afternoon that I overheard two customers berate the police in unprintable language. A young man had died in Wolverhampton in violent circumstances a few days before. The police had tried to restrain him and in the struggle he choked to death. "Ah, telling you, mahn," said the first customer, a man in his early thirties with a neatly trimmed Afro. "These people wan' kill us off." The other customer wore a leather cap. With his mouth full of food, he replied: "Is licks them wan'. The guy should ah walk with a rassclawt knife and juk them one time, mahn. You think any policeman could a hold me down pon de ground an' me no cut him. Im might kill me, but me would mek sure fi leave mi mark, I-ah."

When the customers had left I fell into conversation with the proprietor, a soft-spoken, middle-aged Jamaican. I discovered that he was a friend of the late Alfred Fagon, a Jamaican playwright. Fagon's death, in 1986, had been natural. It happened as he entered his flat after jogging. But it had also aroused heated condemnation of the police. He was buried within days of his body being discovered. His relatives were not notified. I'd only seen one of Fagon's plays *Four Hundred Pounds* at the Royal Court. It is set around a pool table, an ambience which by now I was intimately familiar with.

I learned from the café proprietor that Fagon had lived in

Bristol for ten years before moving to London. He was clearly fond of the late playwright and showed me a scrap-book of reviews of Fagon's plays. "Damn fine human being," the proprietor said, flicking through the pages. We agreed that he'd earned a more dignified farewell from this world. That Fagon, an ex-soldier and boxer, came from Bristol seemed to make sense to me. As I have said, one of the first and most enduring impressions of St Paul's is its vibrant creativity. Men like Alfred Fagon and Earl Shakespeare probably fought against the odds to express them selves. But the younger generation, though still unrecognised, are continuing that tradition. Unemployment and a positive choice not to do certain types of work have left many youngsters with the time to engage in painting, music, writing and dancing.

I spent a morning in a project which is trying to tap St Paul's abundant talent. I was shown around by Paul Harris a young Zimbabwean who has lived most of his life in Britain. The project, situated in the central part of St Paul's, consists of a dance studio, recording studio and rehearsal room. I watched a group of musicians jamming in a tiny box-room, and later, the editing of a video-tape about a St Paul's music festival.

At the end of the tour, Harris revealed that his job as project administrator was under threat. I listened attentively, realising this was the price I had to pay for his hospitality. In a flat, unmodulated voice, he told me a curious saga. A white woman connected to the project had written a play set in St Paul's. Its characters were mainly Afro-Caribbeans, whom she believed she knew well because her lover was a Rasta. Harris had voiced objections to the play on the grounds that it perpetuated certain harmful stereotypes. But she was determined that the project should stage it. She had threatened to use her influence to get him dismissed.

Not having seen the play I felt unable to comment. He placed me in an awkward position. I sensed that I was expected to support his cause without question. As a compromise I suggested he send the story to a newspaper. There seemed little else I could do.

Bristol is the base of Britain's oldest Afro-Caribbean dance company – Ekome. I saw and heard Ekome perform in London two years ago. And I remember wondering why a group of inner-city black youngsters were performing African dances. Barry Anderson is Ekome's director. He lives in St Paul's and I called on him one evening. My arrival woke him, but he invited me in all the same. He is a brown-skinned young man, and has the slim but muscular body of a dancer. Throughout our conversation, he seldom smiled and he spoke slowly, as if with difficulty.

Anderson's living-room, where we conducted the interview, was as interesting as he was, if not more so. A large, top-floor room, it was filled with African artefacts. He had shipped them from Ghana. There were several pieces of carving, and an impressive ornate wooden chest. But even this last piece paled beside a large painting on the wall. An African woman sits with a drum between her knees. Her head is thrown back in an exuberant gesture. She is laughing wildly. Behind her a tree is bent by the wind. In the distance two village women look back, as if in wonderment, at the figure. It is a painting that conjures up the excitement, the energy and the almost magical quality of African drumming.

As we spoke Indian music played from a tape-machine. He pointed out that African and Asian dancing relied heavily on the drum. Anderson had started his dance career performing traditional Caribbean dances. In the Seventies, for reasons which he did not understand, he began incorporating African drumming in his repertoire. "We needed to expand our repertoire, and it seemed the natural thing to do."

Ghanaian drummers living in Britain introduced him to the basic rhythms. But it was when he visited Ghana that the jig-saw pieces fell into place. "Everything about the place, the way people moved, their faces, what they ate reminded me of Jamaica." He was born there. The trip left him in doubts that whatever the company's European influence, the rhythms they best danced to are ultimately rooted in Africa. "You know it from books and all that," he said, "but to experience it is another thing."

His fondest memory was the Ghanaians' response to an Ekome performance. The dance was "Atsabekor", a war dance from the Volta region of Ghana. "It was incredible, they rushed up to us and pressed paper money on our heads and bodies." Afterwards he was told that the Caribbean influence added something special to the dance.

Interestingly, a trip to Zimbabwe, southern Africa, did not leave him with the same sense of satisfaction. "It was nice, but I just couldn't feel the same way about Zimbabwe. There's a different spirit there."

Anderson regards himself as fortunate for having visited Africa. By going there, he seemed to be saying, he found his centre, the source. But for the majority of his peers in St Paul's, and elsewhere in Britain, Africa remains a dream to be realised. Though many are trying to return spiritually.

I was surprised at the large number of people in St Paul's who have abandoned their European names. Their new names are drawn from all over Africa, with little respect for ethnic consistency. For instance, Yoruba first names are combined with Swahili or Zulu names.

One afternoon, I got caught in a heavy downpour. I was, as

usual prowling around St Paul's. Knowing that I was near a community centre, I headed there to escape the rain. Beyond the offices at the front was a large hall. Two Rastas were playing snooker on a quarter-size table.

The walls of the hall were covered in murals. It was a gallery of black heroes. On one side were portraits of Marcus Garvey, Malcolm X, Patrice Lumumba and Kwame Nkrumah. On the other was a tree. At each branch ending was a famous black historical figure from Mansa Musa, the fourteenth-century Mali king, to the recently dead Samora Machel of Mozambique. Haile Selassie was the topmost figure.

Selassie appeared again in a mural of his own. Here he has dreadlocks and two lions are lying at his feet. He is surrounded by figures in dreadlocks who are looking at him reverentially.

I approached the Rasta snooker players and asked if it was all right to shelter there from the rain. They were surprised that I felt the need to ask. I settled into a seat and watched the game, between gazing at the murals.

Both players were skinny, their complexion brown and smooth. They did not speak to each other, but concentrated on the game at hand. A small ghetto-blaster played taped reggae music, adding to the atmosphere. And it wasn't just any reggae music. All the lyrics were variations of the themes of exile in Babylon and longing for Africa. Ethiopia, Mount Zion, Abyssinia and Africa were used interchangeably. One track had the words:

> Zion mi waan go home
> Africa me waan fe go
> Take me back to Ethiopia lan
> Ethiopia's lan mi father's home
> Zion mi waan go home.

We were in Bristol, a former slave port. It was raining outside and, between the music, I could hear the rain assail the roof. I was wet and felt a little miserable. And there were two Rastas, playing snooker, against the background of this lamenting music. I realised for the first time that I, the observer, also possessed an urge for Africa. I had satisfied that urge in 1980. It had seemed arbitrary then. I knew people in Nigeria and for me it was this fact which made me go there. But now I knew there was a deeper cause. I belonged to a generation for whom Africa is more than tom-toms, mud-huts and savagery. It is a spiritual source.

But, sitting in that community hall, I was well aware that whatever I had in common with the Rastas, a world of experience separated us. I had seen Africa and learnt that people of African descent in the West could never return *en masse*. It is a permanent separation. The Rastas dream of a return which is highly unlikely. But it is that dream which gives them purpose. And in the absence of a meaningful alternative, it is none of my business to destroy a person's faith.

I played a game of snooker with them. Then I left. It was still raining outside, and I walked under that feverish Bristol sky feeling strangely depressed.

8. Bath: The Emperor's Old House

Around a bend in the road, the city of Bath came into view like a mirage of gold. An entire city made of tawny-coloured stones, set in lush green landscape, it almost glittered in the mid-morning light. I eased the hired car into fourth gear, and it obeyed smoothly, surging forward, racing as fast as my adrenalin was flowing. The drive itself from Bristol had been exhilarating, but this almost etheral vision ahead of me was my most thrilling sight in two months of travelling. Bath had not been a part of my original schedule. So what had brought me here?

Emperor Haile Selassie, King of Kings, Lord of Lords, Conquering Lion of the Tribe of Judah, Elect of God.

From Liverpool to Bristol, his had been a recurring image, second only to Bob Marley and Marcus Garvey. A Jamaican in Bristol had told me that His Imperial Majesty had lived in Bath for five years. My journey here seemed like a necessary digression, though I neither knew what I would find nor what I was looking for.

I parked the car and went in search of a tourist information office. My familiarity with the British told me that, if my informant was correct, then there would probably be a plaque on the house where the conquering Lion of Judah once dwelt. The British are second to none in their love of plaques.

The streets of central Bath were as enchanting as that

fleeting moment when the city first appeared in sight. Many times I was tempted to stray from my single purpose. Traditional English tea-shops selling Bath buns, pottery shop windows with displays of elegant ceramics, and art galleries and ancient churches beckoned me. But I only had a few hours, and even less money.

Selassie had indeed lived in Bath. A woman in the tourist office told me the name of his former residence, Fairfield, and its address. I drove back to the edge of the city and, after some difficulty, located the house, or villa. It is an imposing building, hidden behind trees, and it is sited at the end of a steep driveway. In fact, there isn't an official plaque. But a plaque, installed at Haile Selassie's request, dedicates the house to the people of Bath. It is now an old people's home.

I strolled around the garden. Through the pine trees I could see a verdant field that rose gently and disappeared over a ridge. From within Fairfield, standing at a wall-to-ceiling curved window, Emperor Haile Selassie used to look out at the scenery and recall with sadness and longing the Hills of Harar in Abyssinia (as Ethiopia was then called). From 1936 to 1940 the people of Bath played host to an illustrious exile. Italy had invaded Abyssinia in 1935, and less than a year later the Emperor and his family fled to Britain for sanctuary. His presence in London embarrassed the British government no end. Britain was then committed to a policy of appeasement intended to discourage Mussolini from siding with Hitler. The European tribes were moving inexorably to war. Ostensibly Selassie was in Bath for the city's famous healing spa water. In reality, he had been ordered out of London. His presence there was attracting too much publicity.

Selassie in exile was still an Emperor. All of Fairfield's twelve rooms were occupied by his entourage. It included his wife, Empress Mennen, his adult daughters Princesses Tahai and Tenagnework; the Emperor's personal secretary, his physician, an interpreter, and a cabinet minister. There was also a butler called Jesus, and a wise old woman who lived in the garden. And sundry Abyssinian servants, who lived in two unfurnished basement rooms, provided the final touch of a feudal court in exile.

Two Bath locals were employed as nursery maid and governess to the Emperor's half-dozen children and grand-children. These English employees were expected to and did defer to the Emperor in the same manner as his subjects. Court etiquette required that any mortal in Selassie's service, on meeting him, bowed and only looked up when addressed by His Imperial Majesty.

Each morning, after breakfast, Selassie would lock him-self in his office, away from the clamorous noise of his imperial household and write letters. The struggle to regain his kingdom required endless correspondence. In the after-noon, he received visitors bearing news of the resistance to Mussolini. A loyal group of supporters were still holding out against the Italian fascists. Every evening His Majesty and senior court members prayed in a makeshift chapel, once a greenhouse, the glass whitened to block the view of curious eyes. Social distractions were provided in the form of tea parties, and private viewings at a local cinema.

Despite his imperious appearance, the Emperor was always broke. He had fled Abyssinia without a penny. An enormous cutlery set, ordered from a British manufacturer – Sheffield? – and undelivered by the time of his flight, had been resold to purchase the villa. In desperate moments the Emperor sold off the family's jewellery to raise funds. But with his enormous household, the proceeds from such sales were never enough.

The Bath people's generosity enabled Selassie and his

family to survive until a charity, surreptitiously funded by the British government, came to his assistance. On one occasion the Emperor was unable to pay his electricity bill. The city's electricity manager personally went to Fairfield. He found Selassie seated in a cold room, his coat on, and a rug on his knee. The bill was waived, and electricity thereafter provided free. The children's young nursemaid was never paid, but survived entirely off pocket money given her by her parents. Years later she would describe her four years' service in the imperial household as the happiest of her life. A Bath businessman refused to take commissions from the Emperor for selling his jewellery in London.

Selassie's exile ended when Britain declared war on Germany and Italy. He returned triumphantly to Addis Ababa. But he never forgot the people of Bath. After the war many were invited to his kingdom. And he built a palace outside Addis Ababa and named it Fairfields.

During his years of exile, the Emperor cut a rather lonely and sad figure in Bath. Every evening this little man dressed in a dark hat and dark cloak, with a tiny dog on a leash, could be seen strolling to the pillar-box. People used to set their watches by him. What the people of Bath did not know, and many people are still unaware of, is that Haile Selassie was more than the Emperor of Ethiopia. He was a living symbol of the aspiration of Africans and people of African descent.

In 1896, Haile Selassie's predecessor, Emperor Menelik, had successfully resisted Italy's first invasion attempt. It was a monumentally significant event not just for Abyssinians, but for Africans all over the world. An African historian, S. K. B. Asante, has written: "After the victory over Italy at Adowa . . . Ethiopia acquired a special importance in the eyes of Africans as the only surviving African state. After Adowa, Ethiopia became emblematic of African valour and resistance, the bastion of prestige and hope of thousands of Africans who were experiencing the full shock of European conquest, and were beginning to search for an answer to the myth of African inferiority. . . ."

Long before Adowa, Ethiopia – for centuries the generic term for Africa – was acquiring a special status amongst those African descendants in the Americas. Ethiopia was an important centre in the biblical world. And African slaves, as far back as the eighteenth century, introduced to the Bible, used its many references to Ethiopia as a source of inspiration.

The biblical notion that "Ethiopia shall soon stretch forth her hands unto God" became central to some Africans in the new world. Ethiopia was seen as the source of the black man's redemption. Some Afro-Americans even called themselves Ethiopians. Ethiopia and freedom were synonymous, so that when Ethiopia resisted Italy in 1896, Africans everywhere were jubilant. A church-based movement, centred around the African Methodist Episcopalian church, and known as the Ethiopian movement gained many new recruits.

Over thirty years later, Africans' international stature unchanged, Marcus Garvey, now living in Jamaica, wrote: "We have great hopes of Abyssinia in the East – the country that has kept her tradition even back in the days of Solomon. . . . the Abyssinians are black people. . . . They are part of the great African race that is to rise from its handicaps, environments and difficulties to repossess the Imperial Authority that is promised by God himself in the inspirations: Princes coming out of Egypt and Ethiopia stretching forth her hands." That was written in 1930. Garvey was anticipating the coronation of Ras Tafari who was to take the title, Haile Selassie.

Garvey was then in Jamaica. His message was preached to poor on street corners and through the *Blackman* magazine. When news of Selassie's coronation reached Jamaica, as Bosy, the Birmingham blues dancer, had told me, there were celebrations. The people sang "Ethiopia, Thou land of our fathers", the UNIA's anthem.

The Rasta movement was about to be born. The Jamaican poor had long been interpreting their wretched conditions in biblical terms. Some people began to see Selassie as God, thus breaking with the slave mentality. Two years after Selassie began his exile, trade union protests swept through the island. Out of that period Rastafarianism made a violent entry into the world.

Garvey, however, who had told Africans to look to Ethiopia, was not at this stage one of Emperor Haile Selassie's greatest fans. From his West London exile, Garvey wrote in his *Blackman* magazine: "Mussolini of Italy has conquered Haile Selassie of Abyssinia, but he has not conquered the Abyssinians nor Abyssinia. The Emperor of Abyssinia allowed himself to be conquered, by playing white, by trusting to white advisers. . . . When Haile Selassie departed from the policy of the great Menelik and surrounded himself with European advisers, he had taken the first step to the destruction of his country. . . . He inherited a vendetta from Italy. He knew that Italy one day would strike. Why he kept the majority of his countrymen in serfdom and almost slavery is difficult to tell. . . ."

Garvey, as usual, was brutally frank and not altogether wrong. But Garvey no longer headed an organisation of eleven million. His was a voice in the wilderness, the voice of a bitter man who was now living in near poverty in London. Other pan-Africanist figures had to ask him to tone down his scathing criticism at a moment when Ethiopia, still the hope of Africa, was being overrun.

Selassie did later attempt to make amends for the errors which allowed Mussolini to invade his country. His country's historical role as a symbol of African hope was formally enshrined with the siting of the Organisation of African Unity's headquarters in Addis Ababa. But his internal reforms were too slow. In 1977 a group of Soviet-backed soldiers deposed him, and he died in prison. One of Selassie's daughters, Princess Tahai, is still imprisoned in Ethiopia. The prison is called "the end of the world". And she is sent food parcels from her Bath school-friends, who also regularly petition the Marxist government for her release.

I rang the villa's door-bell and waited a long while before it was opened. A large woman dressed entirely in black answered. She gave me a fiercely disapproving look, as if I'd interrupted her from an absorbing task. I glanced past her. A few old folks moved about with walking-sticks. Others sat on a leafy mezzanine in wicker chairs, their legs covered by chequered blankets.

"Yes," she barked.

"I understand that Haile Selassie once lived here, and was wondering whether I could look around."

She looked at me as if I were crazy.

"No, you can't," she said forcefully. "This is an old people's home. You can get information from the tourist office."

I didn't protest. Impulse had brought me here. I thanked her, and left.

Not far from Fairfield I went into a pub to have lunch. It was empty, but for a single customer: an old man nursed a pint of bitter and gazed abstractedly.

I bought a lunch of fish and chips and found a table. Before I could start to eat, the old man ambled over. "Hullo there," he said. His cheeks were sunken, his face dark and dirty.

I nodded and smiled at him. It occurred to me that he might have seen the Emperor. I asked him. "Oh, yes," he said, his vacant eyes suddenly lighting up. "I remember the Emperorrr. He used to live up the road, in Fairfield. Oh, yes I remember the Emperorrr. Used to see him walking along Newbridge." He repeated himself several times, dribbling as he spoke. He'd seen the Emperor. That was certain.

"Want a drink," I asked.

He said yes, and I bought him a pint of bitter, and finished my lunch in peace. Then I headed back to Bristol, to St Paul's, where the Emperor's portrait decorates a community hall and can be bought from a record shop, where a former symbol of Africa's independence aspirations is regarded as a deity by doubly displaced young Afro-Britons, who, like their slave ancestors, look to Africa for redemption.

9. Brixton, London: Jamaica Abroad

London has not one but several black communities. After two months of travelling, the prospect of visiting all of them seemed too daunting even to contemplate. And time and money were running out. So I chose to concentrate on a part of London where I had lived for two years – Brixton. I had left there a few months before my journey. I did have doubts about returning. An unexplored and little-written-about part of black London, like Harlesden, would have been a novel experience. And I did, in fact, spend a day wandering around that north London suburb. It merely taught me why Harlesden remains unknown. Little happens there. So Brixton it was. From the start my doubts were to be dispelled. I was to see Brixton with new eyes.

As I emerged from Brixton station, I was immediately struck by its energy. A relentless flow of people created an almost frenetic hustle and bustle. The station consumes and regurgitates passengers throughout the day. It is served by a vast fleet of buses which ferry people between central Brixton and the outlying districts. The countless bus stops are never empty. The overall effect can be dizzying to experience: women laden with shopping-bags and bawling babies, restless black youngsters in tight blue jeans that cover muscular thighs; punks with hairstyles as colourful as the feathers of exotic birds; pedestrians hurriedly weaving through those standing still, often colliding and apologising without stopping; car horns playing shrill, discordant notes; unlicensed street traders suddenly whipping up their wares as a policeman approaches: the images and sounds of central Brixton in motion. Even some of the street names suggest energy: Electric Avenue, Coldharbour Lane.

The area around the station is also a favourite haunt for beggars and the insane. Some days a skinny, dark man in a red, gold and green wollen hat prances about on spindly legs, striking the pavement with a wooden stick; and calling for the wicked, whoever they might be, to be punished. Much of what he has to say is incomprehensible. But he provides entertainment for those in the bus queues. Another unusual but not necessarily crazy man walks around Brixton blowing a conch shell. Arrested once for allegedly causing a disturbance, he insisted that he was carrying on an African tradition. He came from the Bahamas.

A little way from the station I stood and listened to another odd fellow. Blue-black, bearded and filthy, he stood on a corner saying something about Hitler being right. A few passing school-girls laughed at him. Adults paid him no attention: he didn't appear to exist for them. And that was the way it should be, I thought. The man was clearly a racial demagogue. The day people do stop and listen and begin to follow such messages will be a sad one indeed.

Brixton market adds to the highly charged atmosphere. On Saturdays it explodes with life, passion, colour. The open stalls sell a vast variety of food, ranging from Granny Smiths to succulent mangoes, from spuds to yellow yams imported from Ghana, from cabbages to callaloo, from beef and lamb to salted pork and dried fish imported from Nigeria. (There is a large West African population in Brixton, mainly Nigerians and Ghanaians.)

The covered market is a catacomb of little avenues. Food,

general provisions and record shops complement each other. The pounding basslines from the reggae record stores provide a musical backdrop for shoppers waiting in long queues for tropical fish, red hot peppers, plantains and green bananas, and dasheen yams on which the earth of Africa or the Caribbean still clings. Sometimes a person will burst into song. But the market's reggae vendors do not have the airwaves to themselves. They have to compete with the Pentecostalists who regularly sing their sermons in the shadow of the railway arches.

Away from the market, I was made aware of Brixton's historical connection with the Caribbean by a familiar building. The Tate Library, opposite Lambeth Town Hall, is named after the Tate in Tate and Lyle, the sugar company which for centuries ran sugar plantations in the Caribbean. In the two years I lived in Brixton, I passed that building at least twice a day. Not once did I connect the name with Caribbean slavery. That I did so now was an effect of my journey. Another building well known to me also evoked the same theme – the Atlantic pub. The Atlantic is, of course, the sea that was crossed in the middle passage.

The pub was closed for refurbishment when I went back. But I remembered a haunting experience in there the summer before. It was a large, cavernous space, and the wooden floor was gritty. A sad-happy atmosphere prevailed. Bob Marley's "No Woman, No Cry" was being played. And a man in a dirty grey raincoat danced with a woman wearing a green dress. They shuffled in a circular motion, heavy, slow and awkward. She was much shorter than her partner, and clung to him tenaciously. The other customers watched balefully. The record ended, but they continued, as if unable to stop. One wall held a mural of a Caribbean sunset, a bright, warm evocative image. But how uniformly old the customers were! Perhaps some were not so old as they seemed, but they all looked as if they'd seen better days. The mural was a cruel joke, for it was the closest many of these men, Jamaican immigrants now in the dusk of their lives, would come to seeing a sight which had once been commonplace to them. Most of them, their large calloused hands wrapped around fragile, half-empty glasses, it seemed to me, were sitting in that Brixton pub waiting for death. I had suddenly found the atmosphere oppressively sad.

But before I could leave a row broke out. Another man wanted to dance with the girl in the green dress. Her partner objected, and she stood back and gleefully watched the unfolding confrontation. It was as though she wanted to see them fight, to see those two old gents battle for her young and tender embrace. It did not happen.

Her original partner sucked his cheeks, shrugged his shoulders and walked away. The would-be usurper lost interest and drunkenly moved on. Quite unexpectedly, the girl in the green dress started crying. Then she fell on her knees, sobbing and complaining that nobody wanted to dance with her. My drink remained unfinished. I got up and left.

The Atlantic's closure meant I was not able to drink of its bitter sweet melancholy. I settled for another pub, the Coach and Horses. There, as I watched the mainly black customers drift in after their day's work, I knew finally that Brixton was where my journey would end.

Mrs Greenaway, short, box-shaped, head wrapped in a polka-dot bandanna, waddled into the kitchen. Her small goatlike eyes sparkled and she sighed heavily.

"That was Leroy," she said. "'Im on 'is way."

I was visiting the Greenaways for Sunday lunch. Leroy, an old college friend, worked in the Caribbean and was paying his annual visit to London. I had not seen him in two years, and thought I would use the opportunity to catch up on Caribbean politics. He had been detained at his sister's house, and had just called to apologise for keeping me waiting.

"You must be proud of Leroy, Mrs Greenaway," I said, in an effort to make conversation.

"Oh, yes, 'im come through well," she replied. She had taken a tray of buns from the oven. Baking was a part-time occupation. "And 'im look after me good, too. Always bring me mangoes and yams. Bring me a nice jackfruit this year." She beamed a radiant, joyful smile, and nodded at a basket of tropical fruit on the table.

"When will you go back to Jamaica?" I asked.

"Me? Jamaica?" she said, in an almost scornful tone.

"Yes."

"Me don't have nothing there, mahn. Apart from Leroy all me children them in England. Seven of them."

"Oh, I thought all older Jamaicans wanted to be buried back home."

"Not me, massa. Don't matter where you bury, 'cause we all either going 'eaven or 'ell. Me just t'ank de Lord," she looked up to the roof, "dat 'im give me strength to me bring up me children."

There was a profound weariness in Mrs Greenaway's voice, a weariness discernible in many old Afro-Caribbeans. Mrs Greenaway had lived in Brixton for twenty-seven years. Four of her eight children were born there. London beyond Brixton was almost totally unfamiliar to her. Now in her mid-fifties, she had only recently begun to relax. A back injury had forced her into retirement. She had worked as a geriatric nurse. She was still looking for full-time work. But at her age it was difficult to find alternative employment. Meanwhile, she tried to increase the productivity of her cottage industry.

"Yes, man," she continued. "Me too old to pick up meself and go start all over again. Look at me husband. Run go a Jamaica say 'im a go live in de hills. Six months later 'im dead. God bless 'im soul."

There was a calmness in her voice, as if her husband's death had been inevitable. Ten years before returning to Jamaica he had become a withdrawn, silent and solitary figure. Mrs Greenaway had fathered the youngest children. The transformation in Mrs Greenaway's personality remained a mystery to everyone.

"Wouldn't mind leave Brixton, though," she said. "It getting too rough. Too much violence. De other day a bwoy try thief me handbag. Broad daylight, too. Funny t'ing is me know de bwoy mother. 'im didn't know me. But me know 'im before 'im start walk."

"What did you do?"

"Me just hold on to it, me dear," she stood akimbo. "And me cuss some badwords, you see. De Lord will forgive me."

Ten years ago a black victim of mugging was virtually unheard of. Times have changed. The new generation emerging is less likely to discriminate. Coming from the ranks of the poor, they choose their victims according to criteria other than race.

"Where would you go, Mrs Greenaway? You've lived here so long."

"Reading. Me eldest daughter live out there. Me would miss Brixton, all de same. Me is a person who love me market day. Me can't go without me yam and sweet potato. And plantain is a t'ing me must eat least once a week."

"I'm sure you can get those things in Reading."

"Yes, expensive, though. What me can't understand is why dem behave like that. Mugging. And the rioting lawd gawd, is who teach them that? When dem burn down Harris me was near to tears."

"Harris?"

"The furniture shop round the corner. Bu'n it to the ground, mahn. Shameful. A whole heapa black people used to buy them settees and dining-tables there. Give the mahn a little money every month. Then when you pay so much you can take away whatever you buying. It not there anymore."

She was referring to the riots of September 1985. News that a policeman had accidentally shot a black woman had sparked off two nights of rioting. Several shops were destroyed. The more fortunate ones only lost their stock to looters. As with most riots, those who suffered most were the ordinary people who lived in the shadow of such violent events.

When Mrs Greenaway spoke of the riots, there was a sense of tragedy in her voice. It was as though, somewhere in her mind, but lacking the words to express it, she felt that a tragic price was being paid for the decision to migrate.

But the muggers and the rioters and the no-hopers by no means exhaust black life. There are many success stories.

Leroy came in shortly. Relaxed and wearing a beige safari suit, he seemed out of place in his mother's dark, cramped kitchen. He had grown a moustache since I last saw him. It suited him, enhancing his broad, easy smile, which seemed like a celebration of the Caribbean sunshine.

We went to sit in the living-room. It was spacious, and its decorative objects showed a clear tension between his mother's taste and that of his younger brothers and sisters who still lived at home. The plaster ducks and plastic roses violently clashed with a large wooden bust of a Rastaman, and copper clock in the shape of the African continent. Leroy had brought two bottles of vintage Jamaican rum.

"Straight or on the rocks," he asked with a vague American twang. I had mine with ice, and we drank a toast to our college days.

"Man, this place is grim," he said throwing his stocky frame into a fake leather armchair.

"I take it that you don't miss it, then?"

"Miss it! If it wasn't for my mother you wouldn't see me here. Brixton's depressed and depressing. All those guys on the street during the day. You'd think nobody works round here."

"A lot of people don't. It's not all their fault, though."

"Yes, I know. Don't forget after university I spent a year unemployed, filling in a thousand and one application forms, waiting for the postman every morning. Boy, that was a rough time. For a while I regretted having gone to university."

"Not any more, I bet."

"Of course not," he said, smiling with satisfaction, and a hint of smugness. "The mistake I made on graduating was believing that I'd won some kind of race after graduating and after that everything would be plain-sailing. I learnt after that that all a degree does is make you eligible to enter another race. A career. This country really is a bitch, man. You can get a good education. Best in the world, I reckon. But they're not going to give you a decent job."

"It's changing a bit. Since the riots. They had to lift the lids off the ghettoes. They had reached boiling-point."

"Yeah, but look at what they've done. They've created a race relations' industry. Forget it. That's not real work. It's a sophisticated kind of handout."

"It gives people a salary. And they're doing necessary work."

"Maybe. But remember I graduated in agricultural economics. I would've worked anywhere in Britain. But would they give me a job? No way. If I'd applied to some left-wing council I would have got one. But I wasn't looking for that kind of work. I reckon half those guys in the race relations' industry would prefer to be doing something else. What pleasure can you get out of making your race a source of livelihood. It's a prison, man. A ghetto at another level."

"Perhaps it's just a part of the integration process. Maybe their children will be able to enter into middle-class professions where race is irrelevant."

"That'll be the day. They'll have tokens all right. But there's no space in this country for black people, except at the bottom."

"Isn't that a dangerously defeatist attitude? There are thousands of black children who won't want to, can't, return to the Caribbean, like you've done. They have to believe they can make it here."

"Yes, the Afro-Saxons, like my younger brothers and sisters. To be honest, I pity them. I keep telling my brother, who's planning on going to university, that he should get his qualifications, try to get a bit of experience, then just split, man. That's the advice I'd give to any black person born here.

"But that's the reality. I often think that we West Indians are doomed to wander for ever. The Rastas have a point when about the lost African tribe, and all that."

"We have the Caribbean islands."

"Those places? I'll tell you something. Three years after living in Jamaica I began to understand why our parents left. The poverty, man. Every day I count myself lucky."

"Doesn't it bother you, all that need?"

"Used to at first. But you get used to it. Now when I drive past all those acres of zinc shacks, I just don't see them."

Leroy, my old college friend, was beginning to remind me of a middle-class Jamaican I once met. He told me, quite seriously, that all the poor in Jamaica needed were air-conditioners. Leroy had not yet reached that far, but I could see him moving in that direction.

"But know something," he continued. "I don't know what's worse, living in poverty under the sun, or being black in Britain."

"Well unless you choose to, or you're socially inadequate, you won't starve in Britain."

"Because of the welfare state? From what I understand, there's not much left of it. But that's not the point. People don't starve in Jamaica, either. Over here we seem to suffer something more, it's almost psychic. I can't explain it. To be black in a white country, and not just any white country, man. England. . . . Hey, why I'm why I am saying 'We'? Man I stopped being black when I went to Jamaica."

We had another glass of rum and then talked about mutual old friends. Then Mrs Greenaway, her eyes filled with loving pride whenever she looked at Leroy, served dinner. Later we went for a drive through London in a car he'd hired for his two-week stay in London.

A few yards into Railton Road, off Coldharbour Lane, stand two Rasta shops. They are almost directly opposite each other, forming a sort of gateway. Beyond them, for about half-a-mile is a stretch of road that has become synonymous with Afro-Britain – the Brixton Frontline. One day I walked the line.

The windows of the two Rasta shops displayed a range of leather and fur hats, scarves, badges, pennants, keyholders, and all in the Rasta colours. Some badges had the shape of flags, others the African continent. The most common combined the Rasta flag and the Jamaican. There were a few familiar books on Marcus Garvey, African history and Rasta philosophy.

I entered one of the shops. Posters of Bob Marley, Haile Selassie and Kwame Nkrumah hung from the ceiling. The sickly-sweet scent of incense clung to the air. I was struck by the stillness of the shop, as if it were a shrine. Plastic icons of Haile Selassie heightened this impression. A bearded shop-keeper, wearing a huge leather cap, sat staring into space. I asked him where the badges came from. Who made them?

To my surprise, he barked at me: "What business is that of yours. If you wan' buy something, buy something. If you don't wan' buy something, leave me alone."

Had I disturbed his meditation? Had my tone been unfriendly, lacking in civility? I could not say. I looked around a while longer, then left.

Further along Railton Road are numerous shabby shop-fronts. The windows above are grimy, broken. This was the centre of what Brixtonians now call "The Uprising", the 1981 riots. It has changed since those days. The road used to fork, and in the triangle formed were buildings which had become a market for ganja. The sale and consumption of this drug in most black communities is one of the most important single causes of friction with the police. But they can do little to stop its trafficking. The frontline economy depends on it. The drug has become associated with Rasta. But it was consumed by ordinary Jamaican countryfolk for centuries as a tea. It is a drug which heightens religious experiences. Hindus illegally smoke it for precisely that reason in the worship of the Goddess Kali (who is, incidentally, black). East Indian indentured labourers introduced its smoking into Jamaica. Its long-established and widespread use as a tea may explain the frequency of religious experiences amongst non-Rasta Jamaicans. It may also, in part, account for why so many people who embrace Rastafarianism end up regarding themselves as racial prophets.

After the '81 "Uprisings", many of the frontline buildings were demolished. The local council made efforts to rehabilitate the area. An Afro-Caribbean community centre was built. So was an adventure playground. Two new streets of maisonettes were created. Significantly, they were named after Marcus Garvey and Bob Marley.

What the redevelopers had overlooked is that a frontline is not merely a physical space; it is also a psychological state and a way of life. No sooner had the Afro-Caribbean centre been opened than it was overrun by ganja dealers. But worse still, heroin and cocaine were being sold.

In the summer of 1986, the day after a royal wedding, the police raided the Afro-Caribbean centre. They arrived in trains which stopped on tracks immediately behind. The community did not react on that occasion. The drugs dealers, it seemed, by peddling cocaine and heroin on the streets had lost the community's sympathy.

I recall walking along Railton Road some hours after that raid. People were still milling about. And I overheard several comments which approved of the police's actions. That the police had felt the need to bring two thousand men into the area was a measure of their distance from the community.

Further along Railton Road is an open space, also created after 1981. On some summer days, it resembles a Kingston ghetto. Dreadlocked cricketers play the game on its asphalt surface. A cricket bat is improvised from any sturdy piece of wood. A dustbin becomes a wicket. A tennis ball completes the kit. And their laughter echoes with memories of long forgotten Caribbean days.

Sometimes a Rasta would sell sugar-cane, green coconuts and mangoes from a wooden cart. Machete in hand, he would do brisk business decapitating coconuts or chopping up the long purple striped sugar-cane stalks, a favourite with children.

One of the walls enclosing this frontline space contains a mural. Titled, "The Dream, the Rumour and the Poet's Song", it was painted by two artists, South African born Gavin Jantes and Dominican Tom Joseph. It is a sort of homage to events in Brixton and the Brixton-based, Jamaican-born poet Linton Kwesi Johnson – note the Ghanaian day name. The mural tells a story. It starts with pictures of people migrating, followed by pictures of children caught in a terrible fire. It ends with the poet reading his works under a spotlight. The migration is easy to understand. The children and the fire less so. It is based on an incident which became known as the New Cross Massacre. In January '81, thirteen young Afro-Britons died in a fire in New Cross, an area not far from Brixton. The cause of the fire remains a mystery. At the time political figures in Brixton blamed the National Front. Their suspicions were reinforced by official reaction – silence. Usually, when a tragedy of this scale occurs, the Queen sends her condolences, or a member of the royal family visits the scene. Neither happened with the New Cross tragedy.

Out of that incident Britain saw its largest demonstration of Afro-Caribbeans in history. It was a significant moment in the relationship between Britain and its black population. A few months later, the first Brixton riots erupted.

The man who captured Brixton's and Afro-Britain's mood

was Linton Kwesi Johnson. Using Jamaican dialect, he wrote such poems as "Inglan is a Bitch", and "Fite them back". Indeed Johnson's oeuvre sums up radical political mood in Afro-Britain throughout the Seventies, culminating in the '81 riots. That Johnson came out of Brixton is not fortuitous. He is a Jamaican, and Brixton is an overwhelmingly Jamaican neighbourhood.

Brixton's Jamaicanness is important to understanding its character. No other part of London – or Britain, for that matter – has a comparable concentration of Jamaican immigrants. It is common to see all Afro-Caribbeans as the same. But differences between islands are not unimportant. They are reflected in the types of communities created here in Britain.

Consider, for example, Trinidadians. They have settled mainly in the Notting Hill / Ladbroke Grove area, along with other small islanders. The annual carnival held in their part of London is an expression of the Trinidadian spirit, a spirit which owes much to the peculiar history of the island. Trinidad, V. S. Naipaul (one of the island's most famous sons – albeit a reluctant one) observed, is "unique in the West Indies in the absence of a history of enduring brutality. . . . Society never hardened around the institution of slavery . . . there was no memory of bitterly suppressed revolts."

The resultant island temperament, Naipaul suggests, is characterised by "ebullience", "irresponsibility" and "tolerance". From my experience of Trinidadians, I am inclined to agree with Naipaul. Their most famous contribution to post-war Britain is a two-street festival which demands that one submits to the spirit of bacchanal.

Brixton, however, does not stage a carnival. Why? Its environment is quite unsuitable. The houses and streets which surround the frontline are small and narrow. The massive carnival floats that appear annually at the Notting Hill carnival would experience insuperable difficulties navigating these Brixton streets. But the main reason is that carnival is not a part of Jamaican culture.

Jamaica's most significant contribution to Brixton and Britain is a culture that combines religion with a search for cultural identity. Rastafarianism and Garveyism have already been mentioned. Both are but twentieth-century versions of a tendency in Jamaican culture which can be traced back to the Maroons. These were mainly Ashante slaves who fled the sugar plantations for the mountainous, rugged interior of the island. When Britain captured the island from Spain in 1665, the Maroons continued their resistance. Eventually a peace treaty was signed.

The island's early history is potted with anti-slavery revolts. Later in Jamaica's history Christianity – introduced principally by Scottish missionaries – became a powerful tool in the hands of slave rebellion leaders. But it was always practised alongside African religions retained during the centuries of slavery. Jamaica's heroes from the nineteenth century are all men who fought against injustice – Sam Sharp, Paul Bogle and George William Gordon. All were followers of the Baptist church.

Resistance to slavery was followed by protests against colonialism. The most memorable again involved religion. Alexander Bedward is one of the first messianic figures in the island's history. His message had a powerful appeal to the poor. The colonial authorities arrested him after he gave a speech in which was the expression, "the black wall shall crush the white wall". Bedward eventually died in an asylum, but he is credited with giving his flock a sense of cultural identity. His name is associated with ideas of black nationalism and black redemption.

Marcus Garvey was a secular version of Alexander Bedward. Where Bedward looked to Heaven, Garvey looked to Africa for redemption. But he, too, was rooted in the church and Christianity. To many of Garvey's followers he was a Messiah. And Garveyism led to Rastafarianism, the movement whose symbols litter the inner cities. No other religion has made more effective use of a popular cultural medium. Through reggae music it won converts without them knowing it. Ironically, one of the men principally responsible for helping to spread the message was a Jamaican descendant of slave-owners – Chris Blackwell of Island Records. He gave Bob Marley and the Wailers and many other reggae artists their international break. From that moment it began to saturate the consciousness of an entire generation.

The inner city riots of the Eighties were due to the social conditions in the black communities, the feelings of estrangement of black youngsters. But the religious movement which gave most youngsters the ideological means – however questionable – and the conviction to articulate their anger verbally and physically is as Jamaican as Carnival is Trinidadian.

Past the mural the frontline continues with more shabby shops. A few shifty-eyed men hung around in front of the shops. "You want it," one asked me. "Black or sensi. Whatever you want. I have it." I declined his offer and continued up the Railton Road. After the shops, the frontline begins to peter out. Decaying residential houses and boarded-up shop-fronts run for another few hundred yards.

I walked up to Shakespeare Road and then turned round. Back at the mural, more people had gathered. It was a mild but overcast day. The last of the cold days had passed, I hoped. And so did the ganja dealers. One of them seemed jubilant. As I passed him, he said: "Winter over Babylon end."

I met Gus one evening in the foyer of Brixton Library. I was looking at a notice-board. He was whispering to three youngsters. They seemed fidgety, anxious to get away. But Gus was detaining them. I pricked up my ears when he mentioned African history. This had been the theme of many conversations in the provinces.

"You must read," Gus was insisting, "and not that rubbish". One boy held what looked like a science fiction title. "You must read 'bout you' history." His lively eyes danced in his dark, bearded face. I don't know what his relationship was to these boys, but he spoke to them like a father. Suddenly, he produced a newspaper. "I know you all think that ol' Gus is mad, but I've been telling you for years. Maybe if a white man tell you, you'll believe it."

From mild curiosity, the scene before me became totally absorbing. The paper was *The Guardian*. And the article that Gus was displaying I'd read some days before. Written by a Jewish American linguist, it argued that ancient Greek civilisation owed a great deal to the ancient Egyptians. Ancient Greeks, the writer maintained, acknowledged this debt. But during the age of Empire, historians obliterated, or downplayed the Egyptian influence. The racism used to justify slavery and colonial plunder involved a rewriting of history.

The three boys looked at the paper, and its mountain of words, and one said: "Ah, Gus, I ain't got time for that, mahn. We got some crucial runnings to do."

Gus sighed in despair and allowed them to leave. Afterwards I went to talk to him. This *Guardian* reader was an unemployed former bus-conductor, underground guard, factory worker, and car-washer. He came from Antigua.

As we spoke, he folded up the newspaper and put it back in his pocket. "These youths, man," he said, accepting a cigarette, "all they wan' know 'bout is car, woman, and party.

Every day I try talk to them 'bout our history, but they all don't wan' listen."

"Well, you know youth is a time for fun, playing," I said. "The past isn't exactly priority. Today, and tomorrow are all that matter most."

"Maybe," he murmured, "but the past is in the present. See, the white man throws us into darkness. That's why black people so screwed up, man. We is a confused people. The only way to end that confusion is to know where we coming from. Even the white man start admit that 'im tell lies 'bout us. But we still believing the lies."

What made Gus unique, in my eyes, was that he had assumed the role of an oral historian. He had read and wanted to share his knowledge and information. But Gus's preoccupation with black and African history is widespread in Britain's black communities. There is a belief that whites have stolen black people's history. So in black bookshops you will find an abundance of books about African and black history. Most originate from the United States. Some are nothing more than the idealistic rantings of Afro-American historians who have inverted white imperial history. The past is glorified, and everything good is attributed to Africa. Others are thoroughly researched scholarly works, some of which the *Guardian* article quoted.

The notion of a stolen history is such a persistent theme in black political consciousness that it has inspired actual physical attempts to reclaim that history. In 1985, a group of Rastas were arraigned before a London court for stealing rare books from the British Library. The thefts were carried out over two years, and books valued at thousands of pounds were stolen. Their black counsel argued in their defence that the books had been stolen from Ethiopia by British colonial plunderers. An academic expert from the London School of

Oriental and African studies gave evidence for the defence. The Rastas, however, were found guilty.

The stolen history theme is not without validity. The British are obsessive collectors of antiquities and objects of art. During the colonial years vast collections were amassed by individuals and institutions. The most famous and the longest attempt to reclaim one of those artefacts is the case of the Elgin Marbles, taken from Greece in the nineteenth century.

Since their independence many African countries have requested the return of their cultural artefacts removed during the colonial years. The famous Benin Ivory Mask, for example, is to Nigeria what the Elgin Marbles is to Greece. Unsuccessful attempts to reclaim it have in the past soured relations between Nigeria and Britain. It has become a powerful symbol of that country's lost cultural heritage. India was also affected. I recall watching a television interview with an Indian passionate about his country's culture. Conducted in a British Museum warehouse, he was surrounded by crates containing the objects. British Museum officials insist that their collections were legally acquired. If by this they mean under colonial law, they are undoubtedly right. A stronger argument is that Britain possesses the best storage facilities for ensuring the artefacts' preservation. Who or what they are being preserved for is never made clear. Occasionally, the artefacts are displayed to the public as examples of "ethnic" or "primitive" art. The British colonial mentality offends even when it is being complimentary.

As I listened to Gus, it occurred to me that Britain could return some of these objects without them leaving her shores. People of African and Asian descent are now a part of Britain. Their culture is already reflected in high-street supermarkets, ever increasingly in the media, and school curricula. Most British cities are multi-cultural and multi-racial, however poor relations between the peoples. My conversation with Gus led me to an inescapable conclusion. Britain needs African and Asian museums and art galleries. Asians may not feel the same burning need for cultural representations of their past as much as Afro-Caribbeans. They have never been so forcefully severed from their cultural source. But they too, especially later generations, would benefit. For many Afro-Caribbeans it would satisfy a soul-felt hunger. A people of West African origin, the Afro-Caribbeans' past was darkened and hidden first by the brutal displacement of slavery, and later by colonial ideology. Since the late seventies there has been an upsurge in cultural activities aimed at reclaiming that past. But in community surroundings alone, it can appear like a subversive activity, a pursuit opposed to being British.

The Afro-Caribbeans' right to their history should be given official sanction. The great museums and art galleries of Britain need to be seen to be celebrating it, too. Until the Afro-Caribbeans' history is made publicly available, its discovery is likely to be accompanied by resentment and anger. Some of the artefacts buried in museums could help the emergent Afro-Briton's process of self-discovery to be a somewhat less painful experience than has been that of the first generation's.

While the ashes of the old Brixton still smoulder, a new Brixton is emerging. It consists of young, upwardly mobile professionals for whom the area's quaint terraced houses – built as artisan's dwellings – are irresistibly cheap. White bohemians attracted by Brixton's notoriety and black cultures are also among the new settlers. And with ambitious black Brixtonians fleeing the inner city nightmare for the anonymity and peaceful security of suburbia, Brixton's gentrification is well on the way.

But this is a time of transition. For now, the new residents, wine drinkers in Habitat-furnished houses adorned with glossy Athena prints, must co-exist with the old Brixton of obstreperous, proud, middle-aged Jamaican women, menacing-looking black youths, and the pounding bass-filled sounds of reggae music on Saturday nights and Sunday mornings. It is not always a harmonious marriage.

One Sunday afternoon I lunched with some new Brixtonians. My hosts were Kunle and Stephanie. Born in Nigeria, he had lived in England since the age of eight. He was slim, evenly dark and solemn-faced. He was a school teacher, she worked in public relations.

Her movements were graceful, and she spoke with a traceless, well-educated accent. Both claimed aristocratic connections, Kunle from the royal court of Abeokuta in Nigeria. His father had sent him to England to acquire an education which should have guaranteed him a place in the newly independent nation. After years in England he went back to a Nigeria in the chaotically ecstatic throes of an oil boom. He decided that England's orderliness was far more preferable. Stephanie's grandfather came from a White Russian family. She had grown up in the west country. She had been mugged twice. And hours before rioting erupted in September 1985, a gang of youths chased her almost as far as her front door. Despite these frightening experiences she liked Brixton.

"It's so different from where I grew up," she told me. "It's like living in another country." In another age, I suspected, Stephanie would have worked in the colonies, just for the excitement. But the colonies are here now, in the inner cities, a train ride away.

Kunle had far less admiration for Brixton. In his first Brixton summer, he woke up one morning to discover that his greenhouse of tomatoes had been raided. All the plants had been stolen. Why would anyone want to steal tomato plants? His elderly Jamaican neighbour offered a plausible explanation. From a distance the plants bear a resemblance to ganja plants. The thieves, who probably lived a few houses away, had mistaken the worthless crop for some earnings on the frontline.

Kunle was looking forward to the day when he could leave Brixton. He and Stephanie were planning a family and Brixton, in his view, "is the worst possible place to bring up children". In fact, he was not sure whether Britain, as a whole, was the best place to bring up children who are not white. "This country makes too many people hung up on their race. West Indians," Kunle said, "lack ambition and drive. They believe that England owes them a living, and when it is not forthcoming they take to the streets in an orgy of burning and looting." Remarkable, I thought, this almost Home Counties conservatism coming from an African prince temporarily resident in Brixton.

I counter-argued that, as a general principle, people who migrate tend to be the most ambitious and robust of a discontented population. The lazy ones, on the whole, stay put. West Indians were no exception.

I felt the need to defend my fellow Afro-Caribbeans. Kunle's disparaging comment hinted at class snobbery. I sensed, though, that it also had something to do with him being an African. For some Africans the West Indian's past has left him indelibly tainted. A Jamaican friend once told me a revealing story about his attempt to chat up a Nigerian girl. She rebuffed him, saying she would never be seen with an "Irikay" man, meaning, in Yoruba, a sugarcane-cutter.

But many Afro-Caribbeans hold Africans in contempt. I first discovered this at university. A Zimbabwean friend and I dated two girls from the local Caribbean community. At the discothèque one of the girls adamantly refused to dance with my friend. Her reason: because he was an African (the same girl, I understand, now lives with a Rasta).

Kunle half-recanted and said that West Indians were not his favourite people at the moment. A fellow Nigerian and close friend had recently had a bad experience with a Jamaican. The friend had lost his English girlfriend to a Jamaican by the name of Bigga. The girlfriend had met Bigga in a pub, during the friend's absence from the country, and he had taken her to a blues dance, which, it seemed, had completely seduced her. She now lived with Bigga in a council flat, and there were rumours that he had put her on the streets to work for him. Meanwhile the abandoned lover was extremely distraught.

In Kunle I saw the vast difference between the Afro-Caribbean and the African. An African's consciousness is centred mainly around his own ethnic group. In Kunle's instance, Yorubas. Africa, to many Africans, is only an idea. And he relates to that idea through his ethnic group, with its own language, then through his national identity. The unfortunate Afro-Caribbean, four hundred years removed from the continent, searching for a cultural identity, claims the whole of Africa. Furthermore, he claims an Africa of the past, a stagnant Africa, an Africa trapped in antiquity. And he does all this by denying non-African influences in his culture.

We were later joined by Kunle and Stephanie's sole tenant. Roger was a pale effeminate young man with a Peter Pan-like agelessness about him. He was a Brixton politico.

He worked for local government and belonged to the Labour Party.

What had brought him to Brixton? His job apart, he thought it was a great area. "This is the new Britain," he said, bubbling with enthusiasm. "A multi-cultural, multi-racial nation in the making. It's not perfect yet. Far from it. It's no using tinkering around with capitalism like Kinnock and his cronies are proposing. Until capitalism goes, racism will thrive. The capitalists need it to divide the workers."

Roger, I learnt, was born in a Yorkshire mining village. From his local grammar school he attended a redbrick university, where he read politics and sociology. He had lived in Brixton for eighteen months, and every Saturday, regardless of the weather, he spent four hours in Brixton, selling *Militant*, the weekly newspaper of the Militant Tendency.

"Black people," he argued with religious fervour, "are the most rebellious part of the working class". It was the Labour Party's due to organise and channel their "natural" (his actual word) instinct for protests towards the socialist revolution.

I was tempted to correct him and suggest "protest culture", but I felt weary. I'd heard too many fanatics over the past two months. We were sitting in the garden. I doubted that his landlord agreed with him, but never found out because Kunle maintained a diplomatic silence. He pretended to be concerned about an ailing rose bush that was plagued with greenfly.

After lunch Kunle, Stephanie and I – Roger had dashed off to a political meeting – strolled through Brockwell Park. It is a lovely park with long winding paths leading up to what must have once been a lordly residence. In the spring sunlight it looked like a drawing from a fairy tale. From the summit I could see Big Ben and the City of London's outline, the nation's political and financial centres. A haze swiftly descended, obscuring the delightful view. Perhaps Stephanie was right, I thought: Brixton is like another country.

It is a wet Friday night. I am seated in a café on Railton Road. Its interior is steamy and bleak. Its tawdry tables and chairs are all occupied by middle-aged, Jamaican men. A few lonely diners eat in silence, slowly, as if determined to defer the day's demise. In a corner near the counter, a garrulous group discuss Jamaican politics. The man behind the counter, part-Chinese, part-African, a Jamaican, occasionally throws in his opinions. The sound from a television set fills the brief lulls in their conversation.

My companion is Chisholm. He is concentrating on a bowl of soup. We had met half-an-hour earlier and decided to escape the weather and pass some time in the café. It was an opportune encounter. Chisholm, a casual acquaintance, is broke. The meal is on me.

"Long time since I eat this kind of food," says Chisholm, without looking up. He plunges his spoon into a piece of yam. "My woman born here. Don't know nothing 'bout 'back-ah-yard' food. Spuds every day, man."

A trailer for an Alf Garnett programme appears on the television. The café pundits take a lively interest. A man who had up until now been relatively quiet kicks off. A disgusted look on his weary face, he sucks his cheeks and says: "Me can't understand why dem put such a miserable ol' man pon the television."

"Somebody should wring 'im neck," another man says,

locking and twisting his hands, as if holding a live chicken. "'Im chat so much rubbish."

"Waste of energy, mahn. 'Im so miserable, 'im should take 'im own life."

"'Im wouldn't do that, mahn, 'cause 'im know they wouldn't let 'im in heaven."

Chisholm finishes his meal and we decide to leave. I pay for it. Feeling thirsty I suggest we go for a beer.

"So long's you're buying," Chisholm says guardedly. Through the fine drizzle we walk towards a pub on Coldharbour Lane.

The pub entrance is crowded with men and boys. All are dressed in drab, greyish clothes, blending into the shadows. They eye us circumspectly. Chisholm, hand in pocket, shoulders hunched, goes first.

"Mahn, cool?" one of the men enquires, moving aside to allow him passage.

"Yeah, yeah. Cool and cold, Rasta," says Chisholm.

A wave of heat laden with the pungent odour of beer and cigarette smoke slaps my face. My eyes begin to water. I blink and clear them. The pub is filled to capacity with a rich mixture of peoples. I squeeze through the crowd to the bar. It is a while before I am served by a waif-like barmaid. Handing Chisholm his drink, he tells me he has seen someone who owes him money. Reluctant to follow, I decide to find a space to have my drink in peace.

Chisholm returns beaming like a bingo winner. He has retrieved part, but not all, of the money owed him. We stay until closing time. Leaving the pub, Chisholm suggests we visit a blues. We head up Railton Road, passing two pairs of policemen. I try to close my ears to the sound of police sirens which always seem to punctuate the night air.

Chisholm seems happier than his earlier incarnation. "I

was really feeling the pressure," he tells me. Chisholm is a house painter and decorator. He has not worked for over a week. He now walks with a slight bounce, and I believe I hear him whistling, whistling in the rain.

Our journey takes us along the frontline. A ganja dealer solicits us. Chisholm refuses, saying: "Not tonight, Rasta."

"I thought the police had closed the line," I say.

"Close the line!" Chisholm says, looking at me, "Impossible. They can't close the line, mahn. A whole heap of guys live off the line. Have to pay them rent. Buy them baby food."

"Then why not get a proper job?"

He laughs mockingly and says, "The line *is* work. That's what most people don't understand, especially the politicians. The line's a living. Most of these guys wouldn't stick a job for a week. But they'll spend twelve, fourteen hours on the line, trying to sell weed."

We stop to buy cigarettes. The shop is like a bazaar, cluttered and disorderly. The shopkeeper sits in a little glass cubicle. An extremely pretty young girl is with him, his daughter. During the exchange, the shopkeeper notices Chisholm eyeing his daughter. He gives him an unmistakable warning glance.

As we are leaving, a ruffled, unkempt-looking man enters. He is shouting: "I wan' them bury me. Let them bury me, is them bring me here."

Chisholm shakes his head and allows the man to pass. I hear the shopkeeper say: "Is who upset you, now. Calm down, mahn."

We reach the blues dance shortly before midnight. It is under a shop. We descend a steep flight of stairs lined with men and women. A humid heat emanates from a room glowing with red. Inside the blues proper, Chisholm expresses disappointment at the low turn-out. He buys me a drink and goes off to talk to the DJ.

The resilience of the blues dance in Jamaican communities is surpassed only by the church. Though anathema to each other, both satisfy the soul, one through spiritual worship, the other, music.

This blues also has a mural. It depicts an idyllic Jamaican road lined with coconut trees and leading up a hill, like a path to Heaven. But this low-ceilinged basement was clearly not designed for entertainment. There are no windows. A small fan keeps the temperature down. Not too low, though. Drinks must be bought.

With the exception of a rather staid, balding man, all the whites are women. They are obese and rosy-cheeked and they clutch inordinately small handbags. I reflect that the rejected amongst the rejectors have found solace and love in a community removed from their own.

The blues dance is the domain of the DJ. It is his kingdom, and he exercises his rule through wardrobe-size cabinet-speakers fed by powerful amplifiers. Once the blues is in swing conversation is almost impossible. Surging basslines flood the basement, washing away all inhibitions and concerns.

The DJ is to the blues what the preacher is to a black church. His sermon is delivered in a rapid-fire style over the music, known as toasting. When reggae music was dominated by the message of Rasta, the blues dance played a central role in winning converts. Black youngsters would follow sound systems which had names like Shaka, Fatman Hi-fi and Soprano-B. Following a sound system was comparable to supporting a football team, and the highly charged atmosphere of the blues similar to that on a football terrace. Dance halls and basements would be solidly packed. Most people would be under the influence of alcohol or ganja. Under such conditions the message in the music would be subconsciously absorbed. Slavery, Africa, Ethiopia, and the condemnation of Babylon were the themes that seized hold of minds that had been surrendered in the blues dance.

The music I hear now contains no reference to Rasta. Love songs have replaced the political and cultural messages of the Seventies. Beside me a couple are encoiled in a tight slow dance, a blues dance that resonates with sexual desire. This is not a blues dance of history, of exile, of longing for Africa. That kind of blues dance belongs to another decade.

By 2 a.m. only the strongest and fittest of the blues dancers remain. A younger group have taken over. Some of them are faces I saw earlier on the frontline, the frontline runners in repose. A much younger group of boys arrive later. Hair well-trimmed, faces smooth, they seem out of place. And they know it. Their style of dress places them squarely in the Eighties. Hip-hop music, a mixture of Jamaican and Afro-American influences, with the latter dominating, is what they follow. Their leader's hairstyle is unusual, short back and sides with a patch of dreadlocks hanging down like shoe tassels. He looks around, shakes his head disapprovingly, and signals for them to leave. At that point I know the rhythms of the street are changing.

At around 3 a.m. I decide to leave. I bid Chisholm farewell. Lost in the music, he gives me a barely perceptible nod. I could see him staying until daybreak, longer, if he, other dancers and the DJ are in the right mood.

Above the blues dance the spring morning is chilly. Winter has stolen back during the darkness. But the air is delicious. I inhale deep and long. A blues dance heightens your appreciation of fresh oxygen.

On the way to the mini-cab office, I am enthralled by a brief and sudden sight. A Rasta, his dreadlocks dancing in the wind, hurtles around a corner on a bicycle. On its handlebar sits his girlfriend, her head resting on his shoulder. They pass under a street lamp and are fleetingly illuminated like figures under a spotlight. I smile inwardly, thinking that there is, after all, peace and love behind the frontline.

London
January 1987 – January 1988